Elementary LOGIC

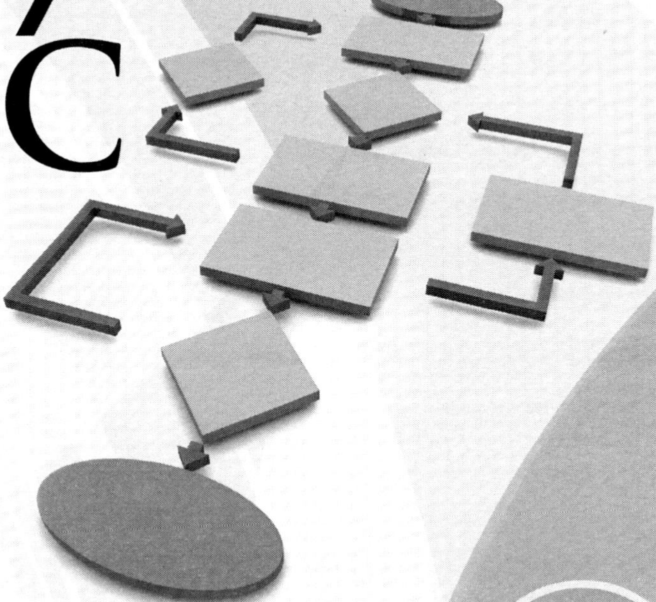

JOE CAMPBELL

Kendall Hunt
publishing company

Kendall Hunt
publishing company

www.kendallhunt.com
Send all inquiries to:
4050 Westmark Drive
Dubuque, IA 52004-1840

ISBN 978-1-4652-4025-5

Printed in the United States of America
10 9 8 7 6 5 4 3 2 1

CONTENTS

NOTES

PART I

BASIC CONCEPTS

CHAPTER 1

WHAT IS LOGIC?

Logic is the study of arguments, or more specifically, the study of the consequence relation. Arguments draw inferences from one sentence (or set of sentences)—the premise(s)—to another sentence—the conclusion. Logic is the analytical tool you use to decide whether or not the inference is cogent, that is, whether or not the conclusion actually follows from the premise(s).

Thought of in a broader way, logic is the study of the various properties of and relationships between sentences, theories, and arguments. **Sentences** are bearers of truth-value, that is, true or false expressions. Some think that the ultimate bearers of truth-value are abstract propositions but for simplicity sake, it is better to think of them as utterances or sentences of a language. **Theories** are sets of sentences. A **unit set** is a set containing only one member, so every argument conveys a relationship between a theory and a sentence. Logic is where we turn when we want to know whether a set of sentences provides compelling evidence for a particular conclusion.

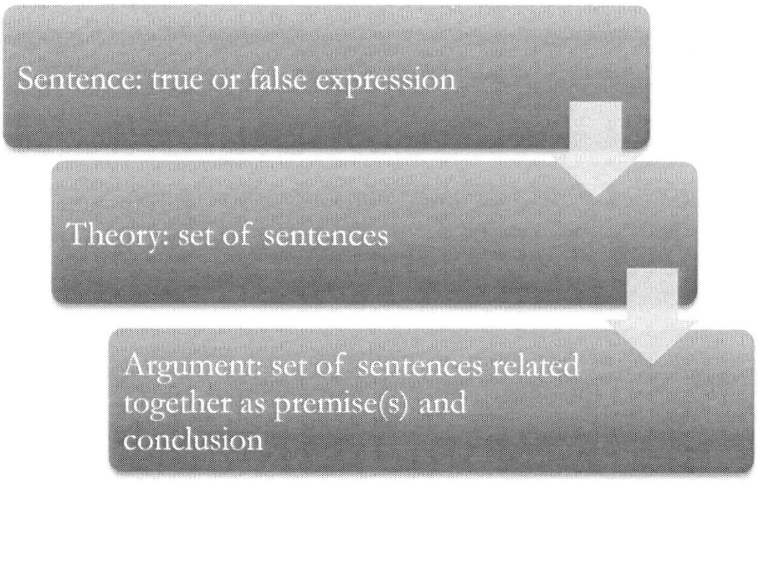
Sentence: true or false expression
Theory: set of sentences
Argument: set of sentences related together as premise(s) and conclusion

Truth and falsity are properties of sentences but unlike the properties and relations discussed in the next section, truth and falsity are not the primary concern of logicians. For one thing, truth matters to us all. Scientists, lawyers, priests, voters, plumbers, and students alike all have contributions to make if our concern is the truth. For another thing, technically it doesn't make any sense to ask whether an argument is true or false, since any argument has at least two sentences; one sentence might be true yet the other false. A similar point applies to theories. Lastly, the kinds of sentences that can be established by logic alone are trivial: all bachelors are bachelors; either it is raining or it is not raining; Joe is a philosopher only if Joe is a philosopher. The properties and relations that matter to the logician are related to truth and falsity but they are far more complex.

NOTES

CHAPTER 2

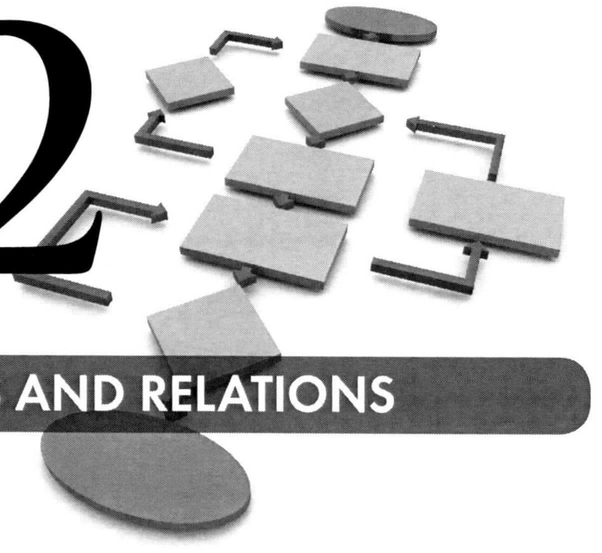

SENTENCES: PROPERTIES AND RELATIONS

As we noted above, logic alone rarely determines whether a sentence is true or false. In this text we are concerned with three additional properties of sentences: logical truth, logical falsity, and logical contingency. Consider these sentences:

> Madonna is mortal.
>
> Madonna is either mortal or immortal.
>
> Madonna is both mortal and immortal.

The first two sentences are true but the second is true regardless of how the world turns out. The second sentence *cannot* be false. Everything, including Madonna, is either mortal or immortal. The second sentence is a **logical truth**: a sentence that is true yet cannot be false. On the other hand, even though the first sentence is true, we can conceive of it being false. Suppose that Madonna sells her soul to the devil for eternal life. Thus, the first sentence is true but it is not a logical truth. The sentence that Madonna is both mortal and immortal can never be true for nothing can have both a property, such as mortality, and not have it. Thus, the third sentence is logically false. A sentence is **logically false** if and only if it is false and cannot be true. Lastly, a sentence is **logically contingent** if and only if it is a sentence that is neither logically true nor logically false. The first sentence—that Madonna is mortal—is logically contingent.

Consistency and inconsistency are properties of theories, or sets of sentences. Validity and invalidity are properties of arguments. Entailment—or logical inference—is a relation between a theory and an argument. These properties and relations are defined and discussed in more detail below. The strategy of this book is first to explain the important properties of and relations between sentences, theories, and arguments; and then to teach various formal methods useful in determining when these properties and relations hold.

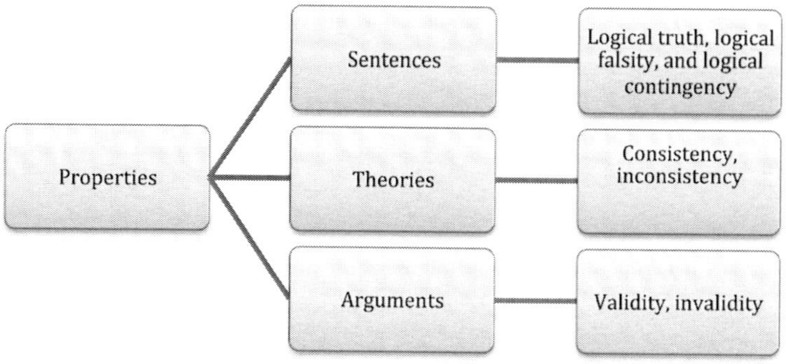

There are several interesting relations that hold between sentences. For instance, two sentences are **equivalent** provided that they must both be true. The following two sentences are equivalent:

Joe is a bachelor.

Joe is an unmarried male.

Suppose these sentences are true. Joe might attempt to falsify the first sentence but were he to do so, the second sentence would also be false. It is not possible for these sentences to differ in truth-value.

Similarly, two sentences are **contradictories** provided that they cannot both be true. For instance, the following sentences cannot both be true:

Joe is not a bachelor.

Joe is an unmarried male.

These sentences are contradictories. Joe is an unmarried male if and only if Joe is a bachelor.

Contradictory sentences oppose each other but contradiction is not the only kind of opposition between sentences. Two others are noted in the traditional square of opposition, which specifies relations between these four types of **categorical sentences**.

A: All S are P

E: No S are P

I: Some S are P

O: Some S are not P

Each categorical sentence can be distinguished in terms of its quality and quantity. Quality is either **affirmative** (all, some) or **negative** (no, some-not). A- and O-sentences are affirmative; E- and I-sentences are negative. Quantity is either **universal** (all, no) or **particular** (some, some-not). A- and E-type sentences are universal; I- and O-type sentences are particular.

NOTES

A:	All S are P	universal affirmative
E:	No S are P	universal negative
I:	Some S are P	particular affirmative
O:	Some S are not P	particular negative

"S" and "P" are variables that range over categories of things like philosophers and rich people. "S" denotes the subject term of the categorical sentence and "P" denotes the predicate term. Below are particular instances of each of the four types of categorical sentences.

A: All philosophers are rich.

E: No philosophers are rich.

I: Some philosophers are rich.

O: Some philosophers are not rich.

Keeping these examples in mind, we can work through the above noted relations between sentences and better understand some new relations, as well.

Before continuing, we should note that the traditional square of opposition adopts the traditional interpretation of categorical sentences. According to the **traditional interpretation**, A-type and E-type sentences both have existential import. A sentence has **existential import** if and only if it entails that some things exist. Thus, A- and E-type sentences entail that there are members of the category noted in their subject term. That all philosophers are rich entails that there *are* philosophers as well as that *some* philosophers are rich, given the traditional interpretation. We discuss this issue in more detail below.

Here is the **Traditional Square of Opposition:**

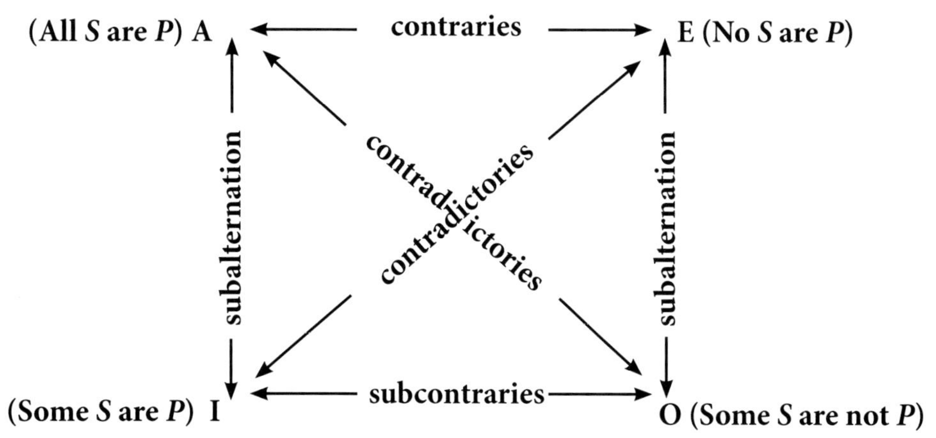

NOTES

As we noted earlier, two sentences are contradictories if and only if both cannot have the same truth-value (i.e., if one is true, the other is false; if one is false, the other is true). There are also two weaker forms of opposition. Two sentences are **contraries** if and only if they cannot both be true. Thus, if one is true, the other is false, but they can both be false. Two sentences are **subcontraries** if and only if they cannot both be false. Thus, if one is false, the other is true, but they can both be true.

According to the square of opposition, A-sentences (All philosophers are rich) and E-sentences (No philosophers are rich) are contraries. They cannot both be true but they can both be false. I-sentences (Some philosophers are rich) and O-sentences (Some philosophers are not rich) are subcontraries. They cannot both be false but they can both be true.

Entailment is the relationship between a theory and a sentence, or more specifically, the premises and conclusion of a valid argument. The premises entail the conclusion; if the premises are true, the conclusion must be true. An **immediate inference** is an inference between the premise and the conclusion of a valid, one-premise argument. Given an immediate inference is valid, its premise always entails its conclusion. **Subalternation** is the immediate inference between a universal sentence and the particular sentence of the same quality. Subalternation is valid given the traditional interpretation. Using our sample categorical sentences, that all philosophers are rich, entails that some philosophers are rich; that no philosophers are rich entails that some philosophers are not rich.

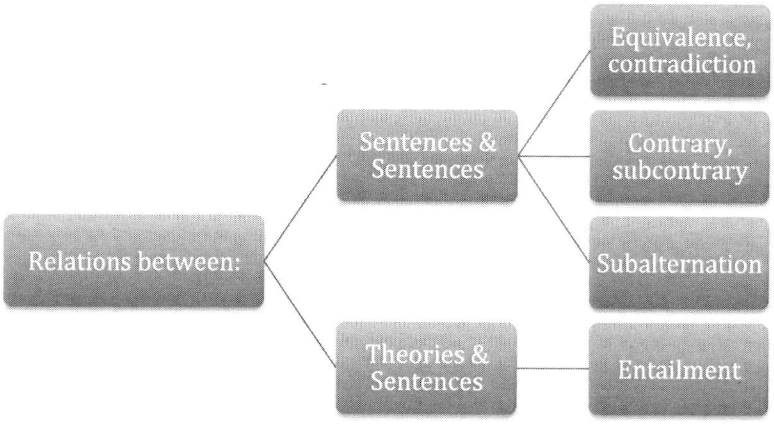

CHAPTER 3

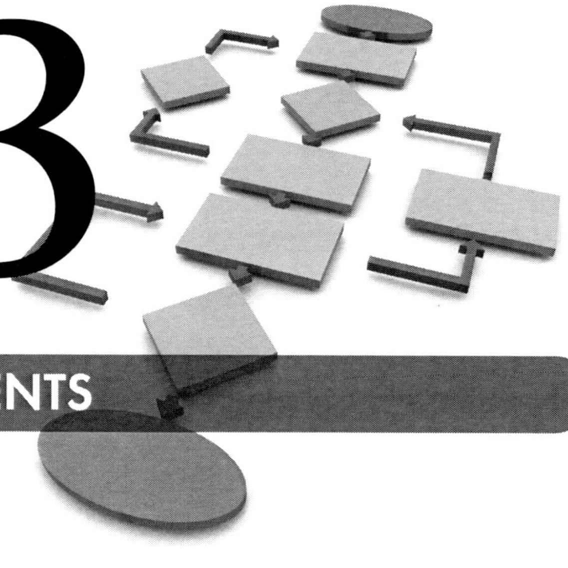

THEORIES AND ARGUMENTS

A theory is simply a set of sentences, so theories and arguments are related in a variety of ways. First, we can identify the premises of any argument with a theory since premises of arguments are just sets of sentences. This is true even if the argument has only one premise. Theories, though, are not to be identified with arguments and, technically speaking, they are not even to be identified with sentences. Theories are comprised of sentences. They have sentences as members. Theories are sets of sentences yet they are not sentences. Similarly, a baseball team has baseball players as members but is not a player.

Since theories are distinct from arguments and sentences, we can expect that their properties are distinct, also. It makes no sense, according to our definitions, to say that a theory is valid or that an argument is true, though there might be colloquial meanings of these expressions in which this would make sense. For our purposes, the important properties that apply to theories are consistency and inconsistency. A theory, or set of sentences, is **consistent** if and only if it is possible for all of the sentences in the set to be true. Otherwise, it is **inconsistent**. Consider:

(B) All women are mortal.

Madonna is a woman.

Madonna is mortal.

(C) All women are mortal.

Madonna is a woman.

Madonna is immortal.

Note that theories (B) and (C) are not the same since the last sentence in theory (C) is the negation of the last sentence in theory (B). Theory (B) is consistent since it is possible for all of its sentences to be true. In fact, all of the sentences of theory (B) are true. In theory (C), if any two of its sentences are true, then the third sentence must be false. The sentences of theory (C) cannot all be true, so it is inconsistent.

The fact that all the sentences in (B) happen to be true is not essential to the theories being consistent. What is essential is that it is possible for all of them to be true. Consider:

(D) All fish are blue.

Obama is a fish.

Obama is blue.

Even if we suppose that "Obama" refers to the man elected U.S. President in 2012 and that it is possible for humans to be fish, all of the sentences in (D) are false but the theory—the entire set of sentences—is still consistent because it is possible for all of the sentences to be true. We could imagine a world where all the fish are blue and one of the blue fish is Obama. In such a world, all of the sentences in (D) would be true, so theory (D) is consistent. The same is not true of either theory (C) or theory (F):

(F) All fish are blue.

Obama is a fish.

Obama is not blue.

If Obama is not blue, then either he is not a fish or some fish are not blue, and the first sentence is false. In any event, not all of the sentences in (F) can be true. Theory (F), like (C), is inconsistent.

In a valid argument, the set of premises (or premise) entail the conclusion. Thus, an argument is **valid** if and only if it cannot have both true premises and a false conclusion. It follows that, in a valid argument, the set of premises together with the negation of the conclusion cannot all be true. For this reason, there is another connection between theories and arguments even more interesting than the one mentioned at the beginning of this section. Each argument has a **corresponding theory**, which is the set of sentences containing the premises of the argument together with the negation of the conclusion. An argument is valid if and only if its corresponding theory is inconsistent.

NOTES

(G) All women are mortal.

Madonna is a woman.

Madonna is mortal.

(G) is a valid argument since it is not possible for its premises to be true and its conclusion false. This can be verified by noting that theory (C)—which contains the premises of (G) together with the negation of its conclusion—is inconsistent. Similarly, since theory (F) is inconsistent, the following argument is valid:

(H) All fish are blue.

Obama is a fish.

Obama is blue.

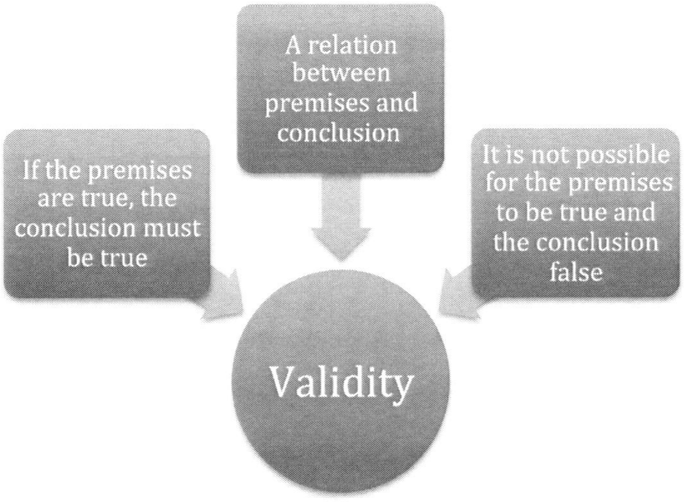

Conditional sentences have the form: If *P*, then *Q*, where *P* is the **antecedent** and *Q* is the **consequent**. Arguments also have c**orresponding conditionals**, where *P* is the conjunction of premises and *Q* is the conclusion. An argument is valid if and only if its corresponding conditional is logically true.

It is not surprising that arguments (G) and (H) are both valid since they have the same logical form. Validity has more to do with logical form than meaning or content, or the truth or falsity of specific sentences. The premises and conclusion of (G) are all true and the premises and conclusion of (H) are all false, but both arguments are valid. Validity depends on the relation between the premises and the conclusion: it is impossible for the premises to be true and the conclusion false.

An argument is distinct from a mere set of sentences in that each argument includes at least one premise and a conclusion, and an argument is an expression of the relationship between them. **Argument-indicators** are English words that indicate that a sentence is a premise or a conclusion of an argument. Argument-indicators help to determine the formal structure of an English language argument. Argument-indicators are of two types: **premise-indicators** and **conclusion-indicators**. As the names suggest, premise-indicators identify the premises of an argument and conclusion-indicators identify the conclusion of an argument. Roughly speaking, the sentence that directly follows a conclusion-indicator is a conclusion and a sentence that directly follows a premise-indicator is a premise. Consider:

NOTES

Madonna is a woman and Madonna is mortal, so all women are mortal.

In this argument, the word "so" is a conclusion-indicator and identifies the sentence "All woman are mortal" as the conclusion of the argument. By process of elimination, we know that the other sentences in the argument are premises, for an argument has only one main conclusion. In this way, we can completely capture the basic structure of the above argument:

Madonna is a woman.

<u>Madonna is mortal.</u>

All women are mortal.

An argument is written in **standard form** when the premises are listed, followed by the conclusion with a line separating them, as above. The line itself can be understood as the word, "therefore." The above argument could have been expressed in any number of different ways. For instance, it could have incorporated a premise-indicator instead of a conclusion-indicator:

Since Madonna is a woman and Madonna is mortal, all women are mortal.

Here the word "since" picks out the first two sentences as premises given the connective "and." The conclusion is identified by process of elimination. Note that both arguments have the same standard form. Below are lists of common argument-indicators of both kinds.

Premise-indicators

- since
- for
- because
- for the reason that
- on account of
- inasmuch as
- given that

Conclusion-indicators

- therefore
- so
- thus
- hence
- consequently
- it follows that
- as a result

PART II

CATEGORICAL LOGIC

CHAPTER 4

CATEGORICAL SENTENCES

The ancient Greek philosopher, Aristotle, is often regarded as *the father of formal logic*, so it is fitting that we begin the study of formal logic with his **categorical logic**. This is not really a formal *system* since it includes a good deal of natural language but it provides a nice bridge between the English language and the formal systems we learn later on in the text. Categorical logic is the study of categorical sentences and **categorical syllogisms**. A **syllogism** is an argument that has two premises. The premises and conclusion of a categorical syllogism are categorical sentences, which we studied previously. Recall that each categorical sentence is designated by a vowel in the Roman alphabet, beginning with the letter "A."

A: All S are P

E: No S are P

I: Some S are P

O: Some S are not P

Here are examples of particular English language categorical sentences:

A: All women are mortal.

E: No person is an island.

I: Some philosophers are rich.

O: Some politicians are not honest.

In the A-type sentence the subject term is "women" and the predicate term is "mortal." The sentence says that all members of the class of women are included in the class of mortals.

NOTES

C H A P T E R 5

CATEGORICAL SYLLOGISMS

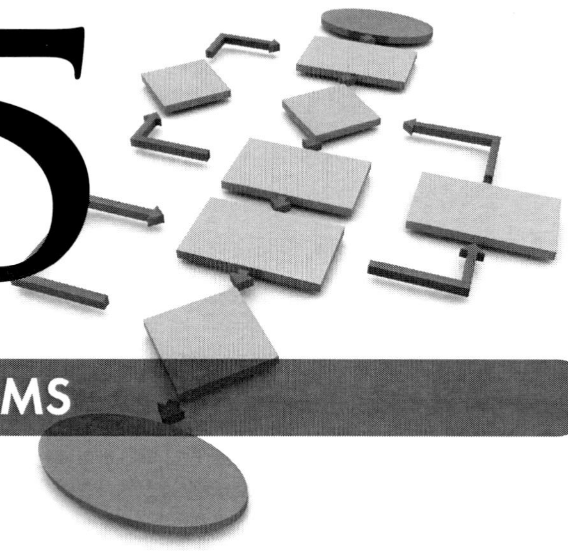

A categorical syllogism is not merely a two-premise argument containing categorical sentences. Strictly speaking, a **categorical syllogism** is an argument consisting of three categorical sentences—two premises and a conclusion—and containing just three distinct terms, each of which appears exactly once in two of the sentences. To get a better handle on what this means, let's start with something that is *not* a categorical syllogism and alter it until it conforms to the definition.

All students are professors.
No students are professors.
No students are professors.

This is a syllogism since it is an argument with two premises. In addition, all of the premises are categorical sentences. Yet this argument has only two terms: "students" and "professors." In order to turn the above argument into a categorical syllogism, we must first add another term. Let's change the second premise:

All students are professors.
No mothers are mothers.
No students are professors.

This is still not a categorical syllogism. Though it has three distinct terms, one of them—"mothers"—appears twice in a sentence and does not appear in two different sentences. Let's try:

(I) All professors are mothers.
No students are mothers.
No students are professors.

Argument (I) is a categorical syllogism.

Each term and each sentence in a categorical syllogism has a specific name. The term appearing in both premises—"mothers" in argument (I)—is the **middle term**. The subject term of the conclusion—"students"—is also the **minor term** and the predicate term of the conclusion—"professors"—is also the **major term**. The premise containing the major term is called the **major premise**, whereas the premise containing the minor term is called the **minor premise**. The **conclusion** retains its usual name. A *categorical syllogism* is in **standard form** if and only if it is written as follows:

Major premise
Minor premise
Conclusion

It is easy to verify that argument (I) is in standard form.

The **mood** of a categorical syllogism is expressed as a sequence of three letters, each representing one of the four categorical sentences. The first letter stands for the major premise of the syllogism, the second letter stands for the minor premise, and the third letter stands for the conclusion *in that order*. For example, the mood of argument (I) is **AEE** because the major premise is an A-type sentence and the other sentences are E-types. Since there are 3 sentences in each syllogism and 4 types of categorical sentences, there are a total of 64 different syllogistic moods.

The **figure** of a categorical syllogism is determined by the position of the middle term. In order to better understand this, let's contrast (I) with another argument:

(J) All mothers are professors.
No students are mothers.
No students are professors.

Arguments (I) and (J) are similar and they even have the same *mood*. Still, they are different in important respects. For instance, though (I) is valid, (J) is invalid. The difference is that the middle term—"mothers"—is the *predicate term* of the major premise in (I) and the *subject term* of the major premise in (J). Thus, the location of the middle term within the first premise is important in identifying an argument in terms of its figure. Sometimes the location of the middle term is important to the argument's validity.

NOTES

NOTES

Following convention, let "P" stand for the major term of a categorical syllogism, "S" for the minor term, and "M" for the middle term. We can indicate the four figures as follows:

First	**Second**	**Third**	**Fourth**
M-P	P-M	M-P	P-M
S-M	S-M	M-S	M-S
S-P	S-P	S-P	S-P

The letters mark the subject term and predicate term, respectively, of each sentence of a categorical syllogism. Argument (I) is in the *second figure* whereas argument (J) is in the *first figure*. In this way, each categorical syllogism can be uniquely expressed in terms of its mood and figure. Argument (I) is an AEE-2 type argument and (J) is an AEE-1 type argument. In Chapter 1, we noted that validity is often a matter of *form*. Since (I) is valid, so are all AEE-2 type arguments. Below are three other examples:

IOI-3	**EEO-4**	**AII-2**
Some M are P	No P are M	All P are M
Some M are not S	No M are S	Some S are M
Some S are P	Some S are not P	Some S are P

From the fact that there are 64 possible moods and 4 possible figures, it follows that there are a total of 256 different types of categorical syllogisms.

CHAPTER 6

NOTES AND EXAMPLES

A. Features of Categorical Sentences

1. **Quantity**: determined by the **quantity expressions** ("all," "no," "some"), **universal quantity** ("all," "every," "no"), or **particular quantity** ("some")
2. **Quality**: determined by the presence or absence of a **negative term** ("no," "not"), **negative quality** ("no," "not," "none"), or **affirmative quality** (no negative term)

B. Four Basic Categorical Sentence Types

A: All S are P – universal affirmative
E: No S are P – universal negative
I: Some S are P – particular affirmative
O: Some S are not P – particular negative

C. Definitions: Traditional Square of Opposition

1. A sentence has **existential import** if and only if (iff) the sentence presupposes that something exists.
2. **The traditional interpretation**: All sentences have existential import.
3. **The modern interpretation**: Only I- and O-type sentences have existential import; A- and E-type sentences do not have existential import.
4. An **immediate inference** is the inference between the premise and the conclusion of a valid, one-premise argument.
5. **Subalternation** is the immediate inference between a universal sentence and the particular sentence of the same quality.

D. Relations between Sentences: Traditional Interpretation

NOTES

1. A- and O-type sentences are contradictories.
   Some S are not P = Not: All S are P
   E- and I-type sentences are contradictories.
   No S are P = Not: Some S are P
2. A- and E-type sentences are contraries.
3. I- and O-type sentences are subcontraries.
4. Subalternation is a valid immediate inference.
   A-type sentences entail I-type sentences.
   E-type sentences entail O-type sentences.

E. Definitions: Categorical Syllogisms

1. A **syllogism** is a two-premise argument. A **categorical syllogism** is an argument consisting of three categorical sentences—two premises and a conclusion—and containing just three distinct terms, each of which appears once in exactly two of the sentences.
2. The **middle term** (M) is the term that occurs in both premises; the **minor term** (S) is the subject term of the conclusion; the **major term** (P) is the predicate term of the conclusion.
3. The **mood** of a categorical syllogism is expressed as a sequence of three letters, each representing one of the four categorical sentences. The first letter stands for the major premise of the syllogism, the second letter stands for the minor premise, and the third letter stands for the conclusion.
4. The **figure** of a categorical syllogism is determined by the position of the middle term.

First	*Second*	*Third*	*Fourth*
M-P	P-M	M-P	P-M
S-M	S-M	M-S	M-S
S-P	S-P	S-P	S-P

F. Basic Venn Diagrams

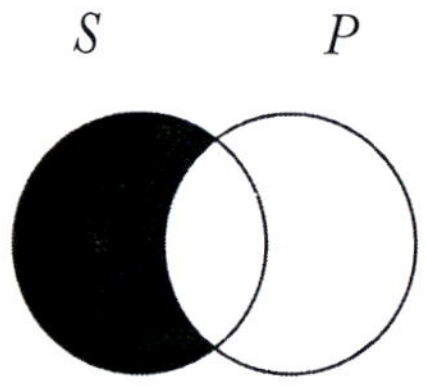

A: All *S* are *P*

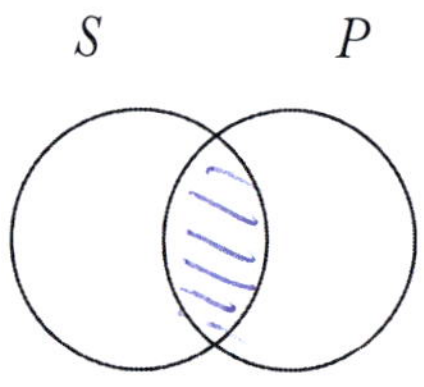

E: No *S* are *P*

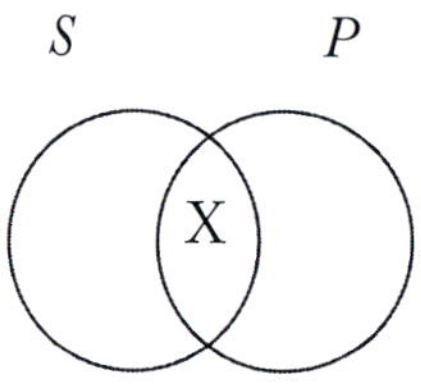

I: Some *S* are *P*

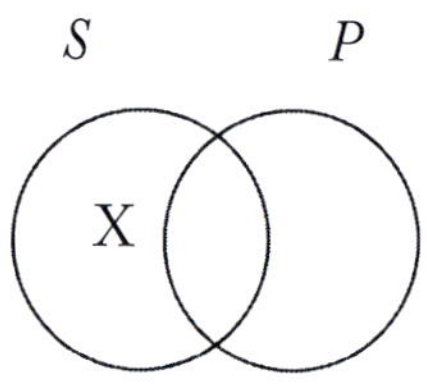

O: Some *S* are not *P*

NOTES

G. Basic Three Circle Diagram

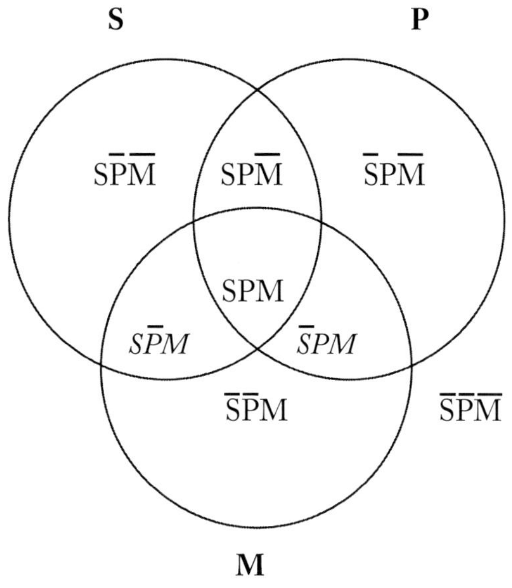

Key:

S = part of the S region

$\overline{S}$ = not part of the S region

H. Examples of Venn Diagrams

All men are students.

<u>All women are students.</u>

All women are men.

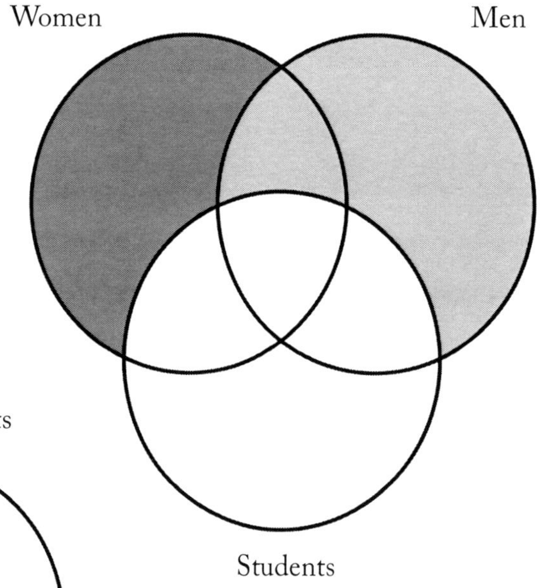

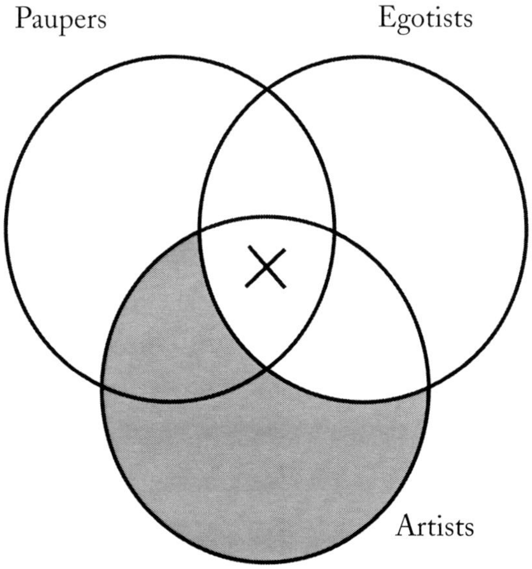

All artists are egotists.

<u>Some artists are paupers.</u>

Some paupers are egotists.

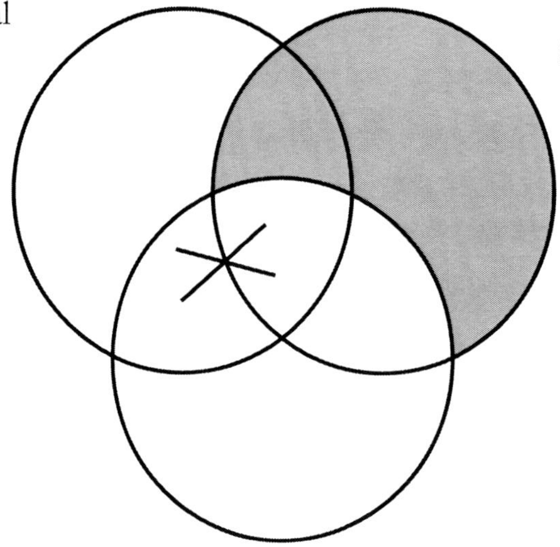

All great scientists are college graduates.

Some professional athletes are college graduates.

Some professional athletes are great scientists.

NOTES

NOTES

Name ______________________________ Date ______________

I. SAMPLE PROBLEMS

1. No insects are eight-legged.
   <u>All spiders are eight-legged.</u>
   No spiders are insects. (EAE-2)

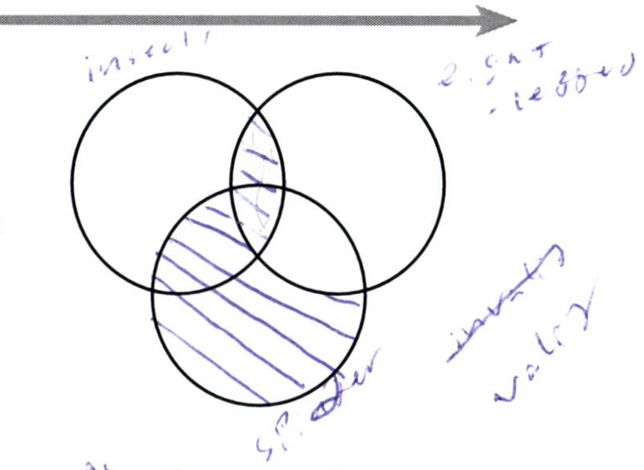

2. All dogs are mammals.
   <u>No cats are dogs.</u>
   No cats are mammals. (AEE-1)

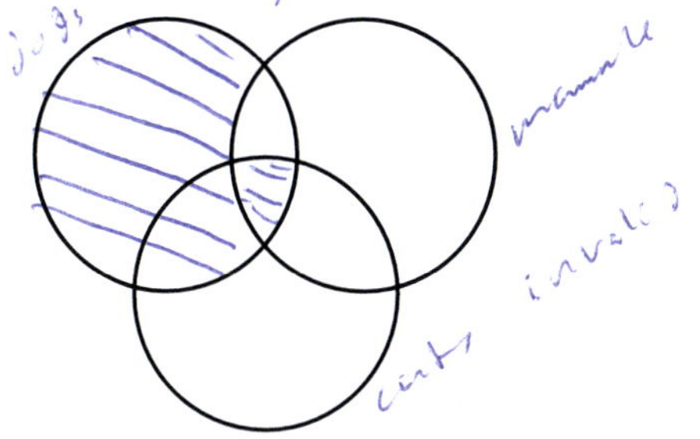

3. All koalas are good.
   <u>All little girls are good.</u>
   All little girls are koalas. (AAA-2)

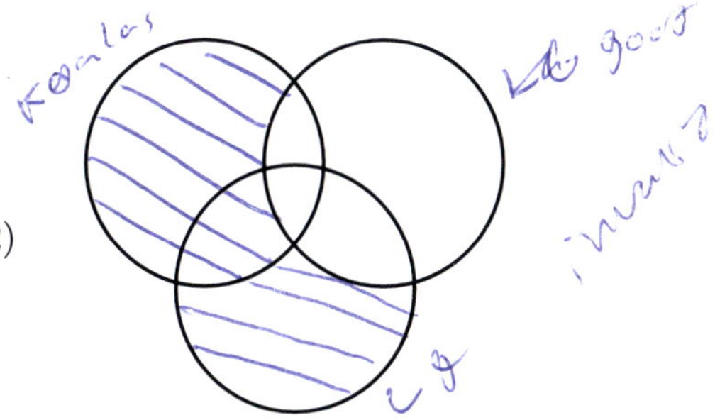

4. All Chinese poets are delicate souls.
   <u>No boors are delicate souls.</u>
   No boors are Chinese poets. (AEE-2)

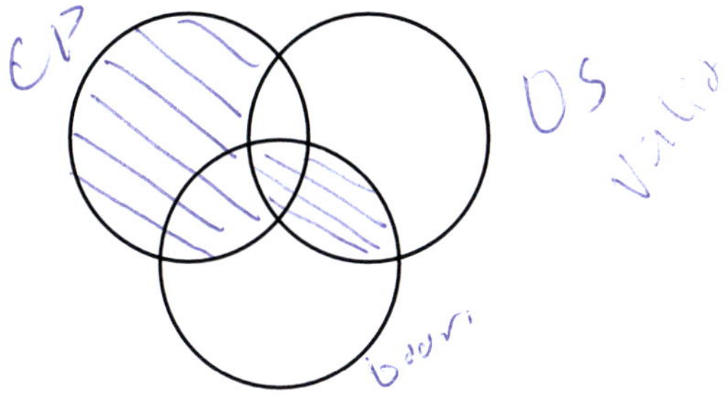

5. Nobody who is illogical can manage a crocodile.
   <u>All babies are illogical.</u>
   No babies can manage crocodiles. (EAE-1)

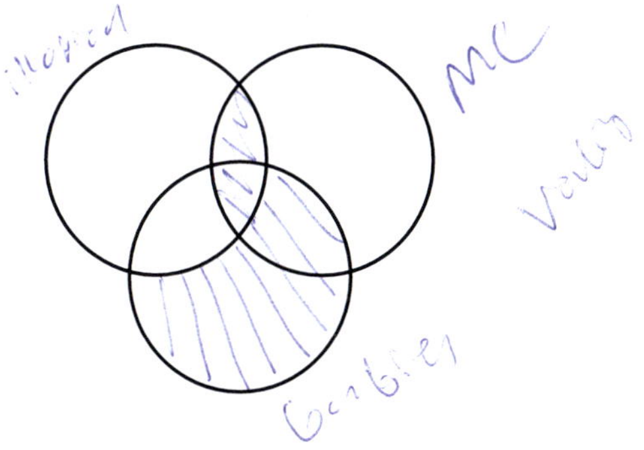

NOTES

6. All who save eggshells are misers.
<u>No misers are unselfish.</u>
No unselfish people save eggshells. (AEE-4)

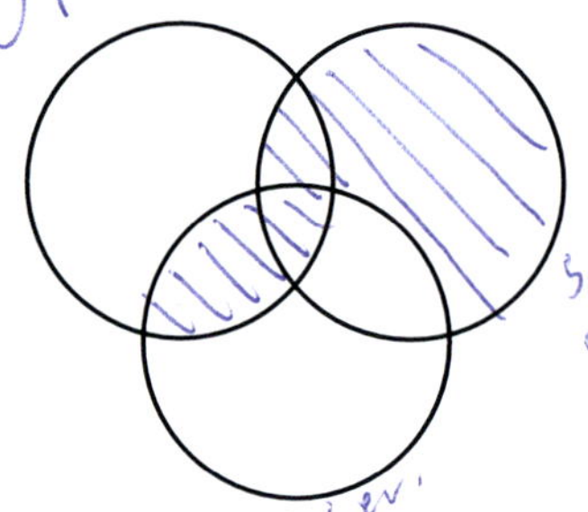

7. No comfortable vehicles are popular.
<u>No wheelbarrows are comfortable.</u>
No wheelbarrows are popular. (EEE-1)

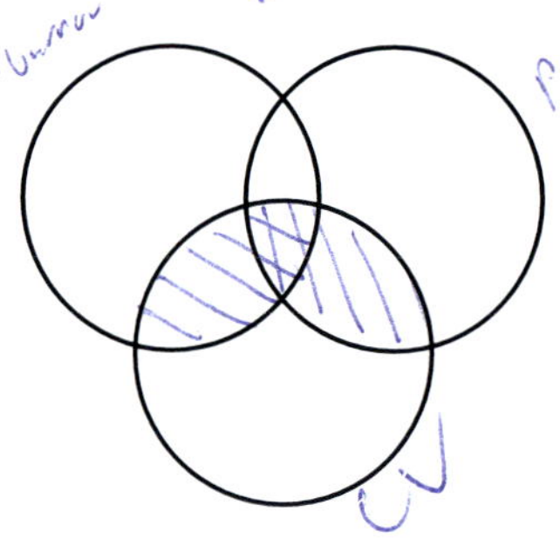

8. No burglars eat artichokes.
<u>All who eat artichokes eventually go mad.</u>
Some who eventually go mad are not burglars. (EAO-4)

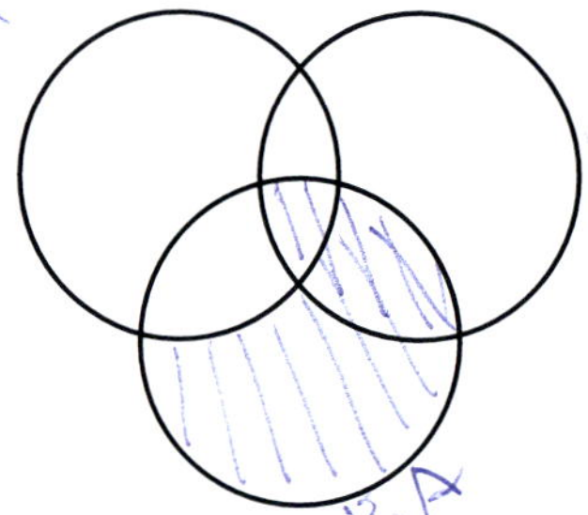

9. All authorized reports are trustworthy.
<u>Some false reports are not authorized.</u>
Some false reports are not trustworthy. (AOO-1)

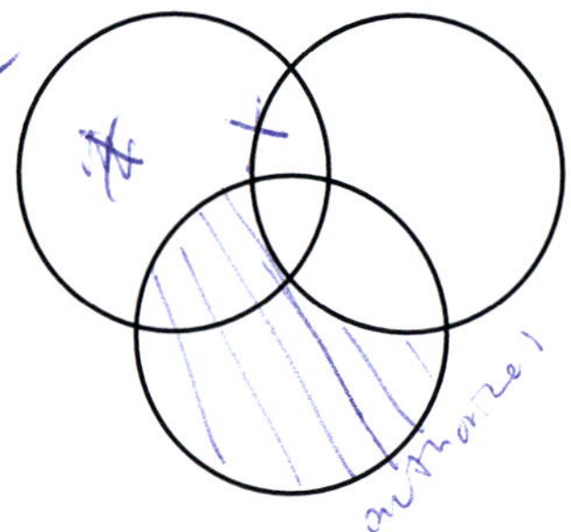

10. Every eagle can fly.
<u>Some pigs cannot fly.</u>
Some pigs are not eagles. (AOO-2)

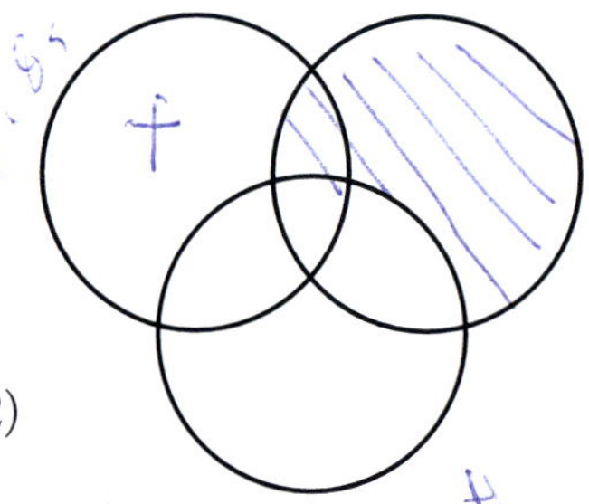

NOTES

11. Some cocktails are too sweet.
    Some mixed drinks are not cocktails.
    Some mixed drinks are too sweet. (IOI-1)

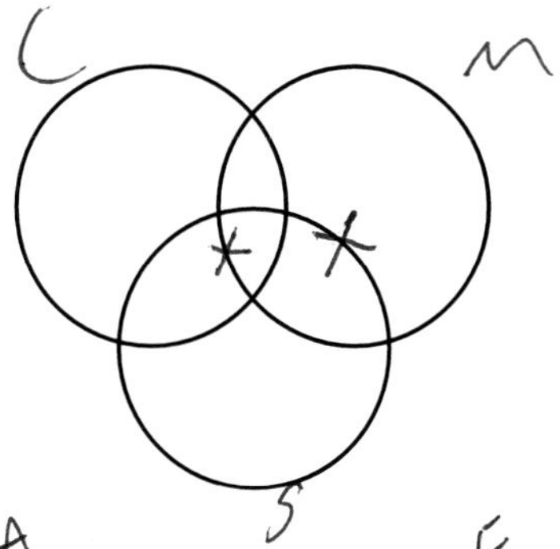

12. All artists are egotists.
    Some artists are paupers.
    Some paupers are egotists. (AII-3)

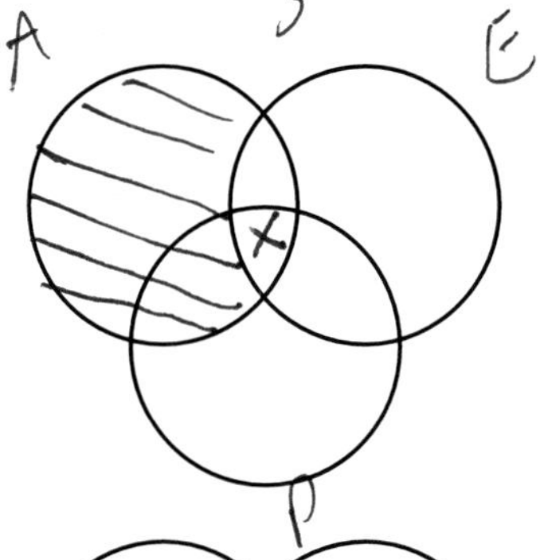

13. All ghosts are vaporous.
    Some ghosts do not sing.
    Some singers are not vaporous. (AOO-3)

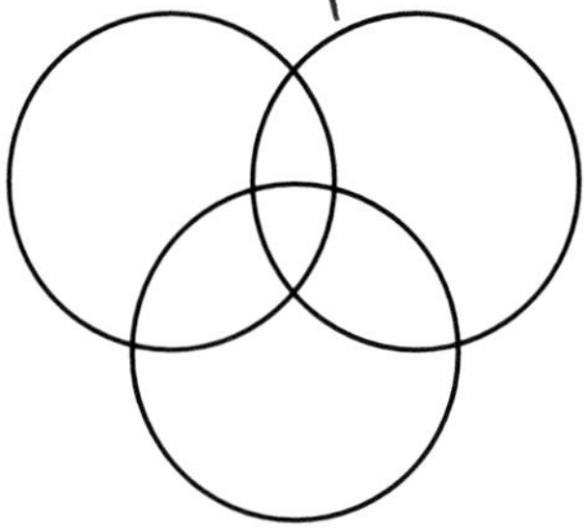

14. Some redheads are not good-tempered.
    All Buddhist priests are good-tempered.
    Some Buddhist priests are not redheads. (OAO-2)

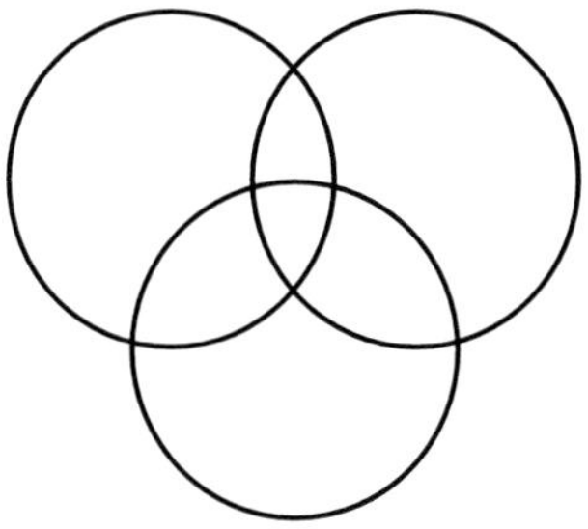

15. All gems are suitable for ornamental purposes.
    Some diamonds are not suitable for ornamental purposes.
    Some diamonds are not gems. (AOO-2)

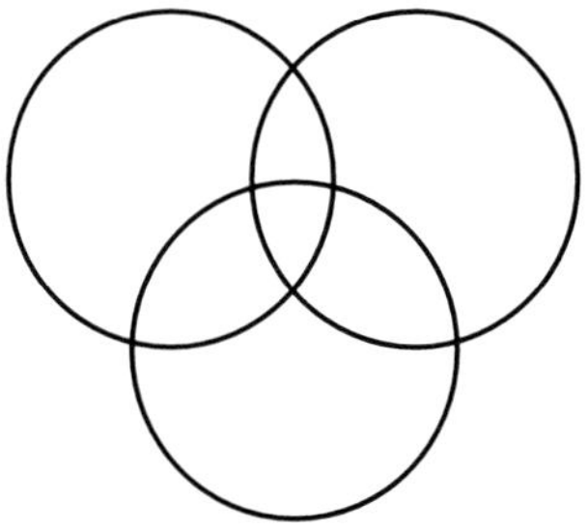

16. Some people stick pins in babies.
All people desire freedom of speech.
Some who desire freedom of speech stick pins in babies. (IAI-3)

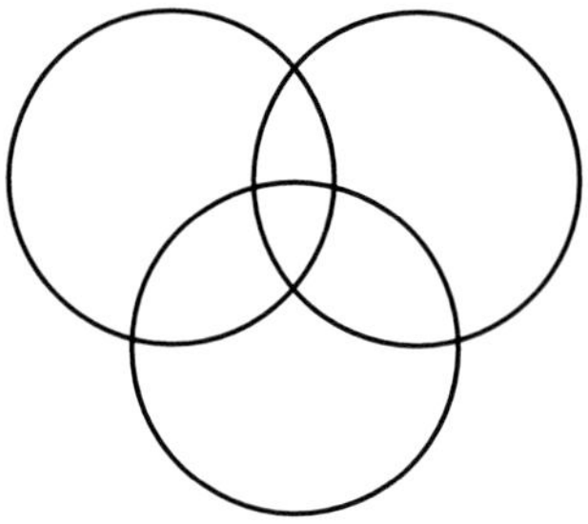

17. All rainy days are boring.
Some holidays are rainy days.
Some holidays are boring. (AII-1)

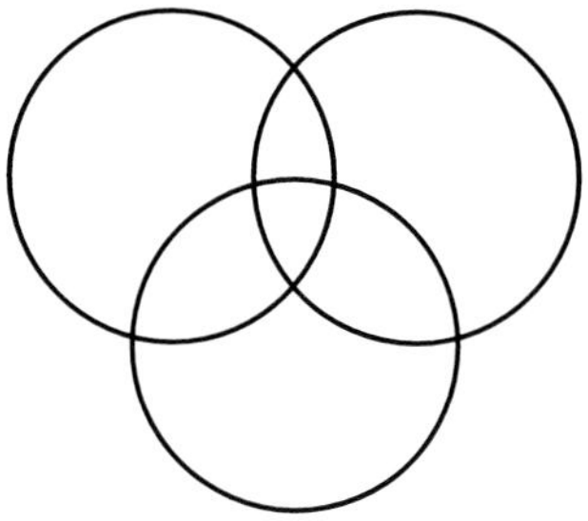

18. No idlers win fame.
Some painters are not idle.
Some painters win fame. (EOI-1)

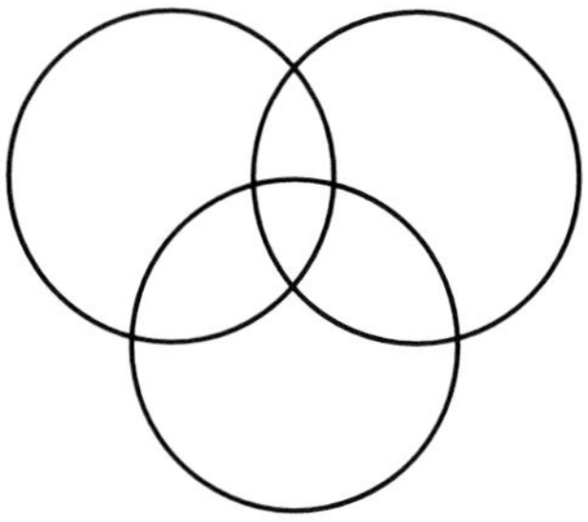

19. No fossil can be crossed in love.
Some oysters may be crossed in love.
No oysters are fossils. (EIE-2)

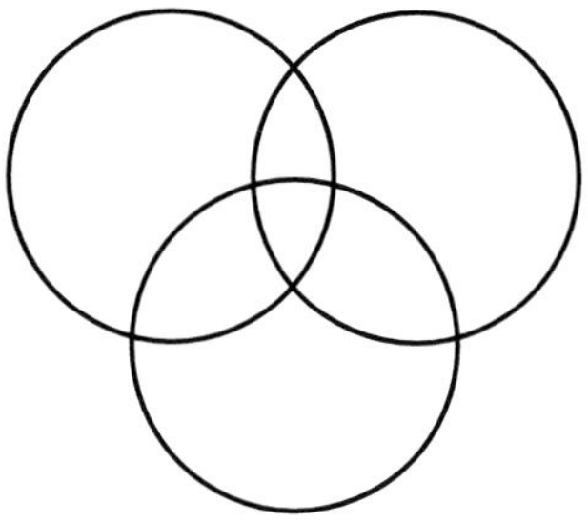

20. No pokers are soft.
Some pillows are soft.
Some pillows are not pokers. (EIO-2)

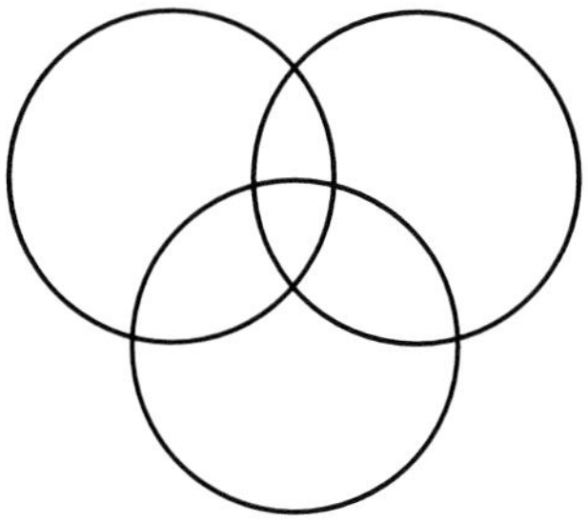

NOTES

21. All sharks bite.
    None who have lost their false teeth bite.
    Some who have lost their false teeth are not sharks. (AEO-2)

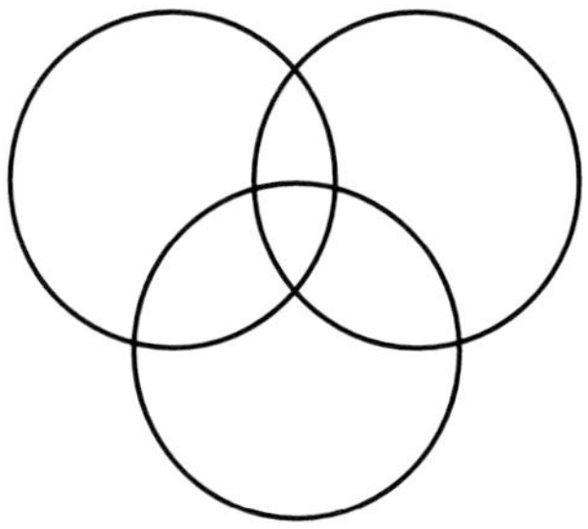

22. Some college students are men.
    Some college students are philosophy majors.
    Some philosophy majors are men. (III-3)

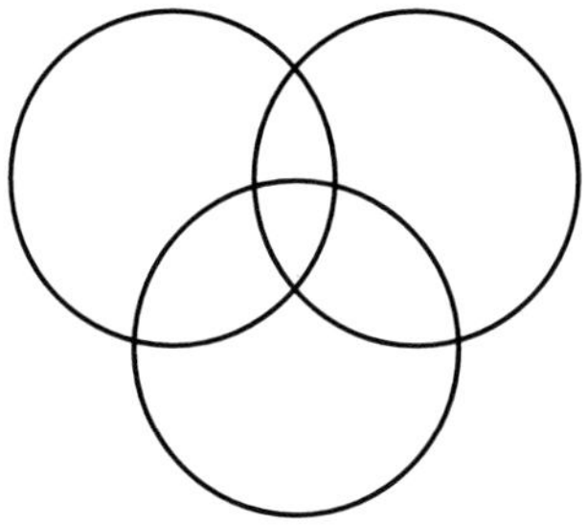

PART III

SENTENCE LOGIC (SL)

CHAPTER 7

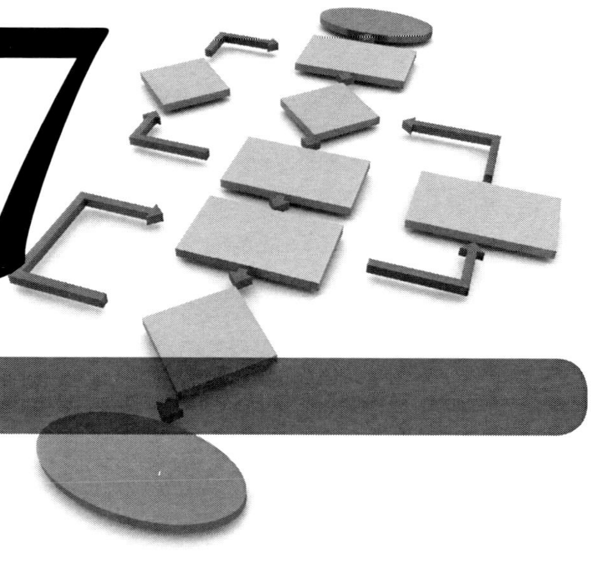

INTRODUCTION

A. Conditions and Conditionals

1. The truth of a sentence, *P*, is **sufficient** for the truth of a sentence, *Q*, iff the truth of *P* **ensures** the truth of *Q*.
   a. If *P* is true, then *Q* is true.
      But not: If *P* is false, then *Q* is false.
   b. In terms of events, a **sufficient condition** is an event such that whenever it occurs, another event occurs.
   c. In a true conditional [$P \supset Q$], the truth of the **antecedent** ["if"-component, *P*] is sufficient for that of the **consequent** ["then"-component, *Q*]. The English word "if" [without "only"] picks out sufficient conditions.

2. The truth of a sentence, *P*, is **necessary** for the truth of a sentence, *Q*, iff the truth of *Q* is **required** for the truth of *P*.
   a. If *Q* is false, then *P* is false.
      But not: If *Q* is true, then *P* is true.
   b. In terms of events, a **necessary condition** is an event in whose absence another event could not occur.
   c. In a true conditional [$P \supset Q$], the truth of the **consequent** ["then"-component, *Q*] is necessary for the truth of the **antecedent** ["if"-component, *P*]. The English words "only if" pick out necessary conditions.

3. The truth of a sentence, *P*, is **necessary and sufficient** for the truth of a sentence, *Q*, iff the truth of *P* both **ensures** and is **required** for the truth of *Q*.
   a. If *P* is true, then *Q* is true and if *P* is false, then *Q* is false.
      Also: If *Q* is true, then *P* is true and if *Q* is false, then *P* is false.

b. In terms of events, a **necessary and sufficient condition** is an event such that whenever it occurs, another event occurs and in whose absence the other event could not occur.
c. In a true biconditional [$P \equiv Q$], the components are necessary and sufficient for each other.
The English words "if and only if" pick out necessary and sufficient conditions.

NOTES

B. Examples

1. Suppose the Yankees are leading the Braves, three games to two games, in the World Series, which is best of seven games.
   a. Winning the sixth game is sufficient for the Yankees winning the World Series, but it is not necessary.
   b. Winning the sixth game is necessary for the Braves winning the World Series, but it is not sufficient.
   If the Braves win the sixth game, then winning the seventh game is both necessary and sufficient for both teams winning the World Series.

2. Being a woman is sufficient for being a person but not necessary. Being a person is necessary for being a woman but not sufficient.

C. Translations of Conditional Sentences

1. All of the following sentences are logically equivalent to each other.
   a. If Jan is in Tucson, then he is in Arizona.
   b. Jan is in Tucson only if he is in Arizona.
   c. Jan is in Arizona if he is in Tucson.
   d. Jan is not in Tucson unless he is in Arizona.

2. Necessary and Sufficient Conditions
   a. The word "if," without "only," always indicates a sufficient condition, so (1a) and (1c) indicate that being in Tucson is sufficient for being in Arizona.
   b. The expression "only if" always indicates a necessary condition, so (1b) indicates that being in Arizona is necessary for being in Tucson.
   c. The word "unless" always indicates a necessary condition for the *failure* of something. Thus, (1d) indicates that being in Arizona is necessary for the failure of not being in Tucson, that is, it is necessary for being in Tucson. Also, not being in Tucson is necessary for the failure of being in Arizona, or for not being in Arizona.

D. Material Conditionals (represented by "$\supset$" in SL)

1. **Conditionals of emphasis** (necessary condition is false)
   If Hilary wins the next election, then I'm a monkey's uncle.

NOTES

E. Conditionals of Entailment (can be translated by "⊃" into SL)

1. **Corresponding conditionals**
   If all women are mortal and Madonna is a woman, then Madonna is mortal.

2. **Generalized conditionals**
   If everyone is happy, then John is happy.

3. **Definitional conditionals**
   If it's brown, then it's colored.

F. Non-Truth-Functional Conditionals (cannot be translated into SL as compound sentences)

1. **Counterfactual and subjunctive conditionals**
   If I were your mother, then I'd make you take more philosophy classes.
   If Hitler had kept his treaty with Stalin, then he would have defeated England.

2. **Causal conditionals**
   If this is metal, then it will expand when heated.
   If this is metal, then it will contract when heated.

G. Truth-Functional Connective

A sentential connective is **truth-functional** iff the truth-value of the new compound sentence generated by the connective is wholly determined by the truth-value(s) of the component sentence(s) together with the meaning (i.e., the characteristic truth-table definition) of the sentential connective.

H. Some More Non-Truth-Functional Connectives

1. Modal, intensional or temporal connectives:
   It is necessary/possible that . . .
   . . . because . . .
   S believes/knows that . . .
   . . . before/after . . .
   . . . and then . . .

2. Conjunctions:
   Gin and vermouth make a great martini.
   Joe and Cindy are married.

I. Notes on Conditions and Conditionals

NOTES

antecedent
sufficient condition
follows "if"

P ⊃ Q

consequent
necessary condition
follows "only if"

"if" (without "only") is a sufficient condition indicator.

- Q if P
- P ⊃ Q

"only if" indicates necessary condition

- Q only if P
- Q ⊃ P
- ~P ⊃ ~Q

"if and only if" indicates necessary and sufficient conditions

- Q if and only if P
- (P ⊃ Q) & (Q ⊃ P)

"unless" indicates a necessary condition for *failure*; "unless" ≈ "if not"

- P unless Q = P if not Q
  = If not -Q, P
- ~Q ⊃ P = ~P ⊃ Q
- P v Q

J. Example of "unless"

Suppose Cindy says to Joe: "We're not going to the party unless you change those pants."

G = We're going to the party.
C = You change those pants.

1. C v ~G = ~G v C
   Either you change those pants or we're not going to the party.

2. G ⊃ C
   If we're going to the party, then you must change those pants.

3. ~C ⊃ ~G
   If you don't change those pants, then we're not going to the party.

CHAPTER 8

SL TRANSLATIONS

THE LANGUAGE OF SL (SENTENCE LOGIC)

1. SL vocabulary:
   Sentence Letters:
   A, B, C, …, A_1, B_1, etc.
   Sentential Connectives:
   ~, &, v, ⊃, ≡
   Punctuation Marks:
   ), (

2. SL grammar:
   - If X is an SL sentence, then ~X is an SL sentence.
   - If X and Y are SL sentences, then (X & Y) is a sentence.
   - If X and Y are SL sentences, then (X v Y) is a sentence.
   - If X and Y are SL sentences, then (X ⊃ Y) is a sentence.
   - If X and Y are SL sentences, then (X ≡ Y) is a sentence.
   - Informal Rule 1: Parentheses may be dropped when they are the first and last symbols written and they are *partner parentheses*: X & Y, etc.
   - Informal Rule 2: Brackets may be used instead of parentheses: [X & Y], etc.

3. Truth-functional Symbols

Negation	~	¬	
Conjunction	**&**	.	∧
Disjunction	**v**		
Material Conditional	⊃		
Material Biconditional	≡	↔	

BASIC TRANSLATIONS

NOTES

1. **Negations: not, no, it is not the case that, in-, un-, etc.**
   Each numbered sentence is translated as: ~ P
   A. not
   1. George is not a wimp.
      P = George is a wimp.
   2. Some philosophers are not rich.
      P = All philosophers are rich.

   B. no
   1. No philosophers are rich.
      P = Some philosophers are rich.

   C. it is not the case that
   1. It is not the case that George is a wimp.
      P = George is a wimp.

   D negative prefixes: in-, un-, etc.
   1. The ring is inexpensive.
      P = The ring is expensive.
   2. George is unhappy.
      P = George is happy.

2. **Disjunctions: or, either ... or, unless**
   Each numbered sentence is translated as: P v Q
   A. or/either ... or ...
   1. Either Jack or Jill will fall.
      P = Jack will fall.
      Q = Jill will fall.
   2. Jill will fall or win.
      P = Jill will fall.
      Q = Jill will win.

   B. unless
   1. Unless Jill falls, she will win.
      P = Jill will fall.
      Q = Jill will win.
   2. Jill will win unless she falls.
      P = Jill will win.
      Q = Jill will fall.

3. **Conjunctions: and, both ... and, but, although**
   Each numbered sentence is translated as: P & Q
   A. and/both ... and ...
   1. Both Jack and Jill will fall.
      P = Jack will fall.
      Q = Jill will fall.

NOTES

B. but

1. The ring is beautiful but expensive.
   P = The ring is beautiful.
   Q = The ring is expensive.

C. although

1. Although the ring is expensive, it is beautiful.
   P = The ring is beautiful.
   Q = The ring is expensive.

4. Conditionals: if, if ... then, only if, unless

Each numbered sentence is translated as: $P \supset Q$

A. if/if ... then ...

1. If Elmo is in Tucson, then Elmo is in Arizona.
2. If Elmo is in Tucson, he's in Arizona.
3. Elmo is in Arizona if he's in Tucson.
   P = Elmo is in Tucson.
   Q = Elmo is in Arizona.

B. only if

1. Elmo is in Tucson only if he's in Arizona.
   P = Elmo is in Tucson.
   Q = Elmo is in Arizona.

C. unless

1. Elmo is not in Tucson unless he is in Arizona.
2. Unless Elmo is in Arizona, he is not in Tucson.
   P = Elmo is in Tucson.
   Q = Elmo is in Arizona.

5. Biconditionals: if and only if, but only if

Each numbered sentence is translated as: $P \equiv Q$

A. if and only if

1. I will clean the garage if and only if Hazel will help me.
   P = I will clean the garage.
   Q = Hazel will help me clean the garage.

6. Examples of Sentential Logic Translations

KEY:

B	=	Bob is a Democrat.
F	=	Elmo is a fool.
J	=	Joe is a Democrat.
L	=	Elmo is a liar.
R	=	Bob is a Republican.
S	=	Elmo is a sex pot.

A. Disjunctions and Conjunctions

1. Elmo is either a liar or a fool.

NOTES

2. Elmo is a liar but not a fool.
3. Although Joe is a Democrat, Bob is a Republican.
4. Elmo is not a sex pot but he is either a liar or a fool.
5. Either Elmo is a liar but not a fool or Elmo is a sex pot.
6. Unless Bob is a Democrat, he is a Republican.
7. Elmo is not a liar unless he is a fool.
8. Elmo is both a liar and a fool.

B. Neither ... nor ...; not both ...
1. Neither Joe nor Bob is a Democrat.
2. Bob is neither a Democrat nor a Republican.
3. Elmo is neither a liar nor a fool nor sex pot.
4. It is not the case that both Bob and Joe are Democrats.
5. Bob is not both a Democrat and a Republican.
6. It is not the case that Elmo is both a liar and a fool.

C. Conditionals
1. Bob is a Democrat only if he is not a Republican.
2. Bob is not a Democrat unless he is not a Republican.
3. Bob is not a Republican if he is a Democrat.
4. If Elmo is either a liar or a fool, then he is not a sex pot.
5. If Elmo is a sex pot, then he is neither a liar nor a fool.
6. If Elmo is neither a liar nor a fool, then he is a sex pot.
7. If Elmo is a liar if he is a fool, then Elmo is a liar only if he is a fool.

D. Mixed Bag
1. Unless Elmo is a liar, he is both a fool and a sex pot.
2. If Elmo is a sex pot but a fool, then he is a liar.
3. It is the case that both Elmo is a liar unless he is a sex pot and if he is a sex pot, he is not a fool.
4. Either it is not the case that Elmo is both a liar and a fool or Elmo is a sex pot.
5. It is not the case that either Elmo is both a liar and a fool or Elmo is a sex pot.
6. It is the case that both it is not the case that Elmo is either a liar or a fool and Elmo is a sex pot.

E. Some Tricky Translations
1. David and Evy are married.
2. If Hitler had kept his treaty with Stalin, he would have defeated England.
3. Some of my friends are not philosophers.
4. None of my friends are philosophers.

7. Answers

A. Disjunctions and Conjunctions
1. L v F F v L
2. L & ~ F

NOTES

3. J & R — R & J
4. ~ S & (L v F)
5. (L & ~ F) v S
6. B v R — ~ B ⊃ R — ~ R ⊃ B
7. ~ L v F — L ⊃ F — ~ F ⊃ ~ L
8. L & F

B. Neither ... nor ...; not both ...
1. ~ (J v B) — ~ J & ~ B
2. ~ (B v R) — ~ B & ~ R
3. ~ [(L v F) v S] — (~ L & ~ F) & ~ S
4. ~ (B & J) — ~ B v ~ J
5. ~ (B & R) — ~ B v ~ R
6. ~ (L & F) — ~ L v ~ F

C. Conditionals
1. B ⊃ ~ R
2. ~ B v ~ R — R ⊃ ~ B — B ⊃ ~ R
3. B ⊃ ~ R
4. (L v F) ⊃ ~ S
5. S ⊃ ~ (L v F)
6. ~ (L v F) ⊃ S
7. (F ⊃ L) ⊃ (L ⊃ F)

D. Mixed Bag
1. L v (F & S) — ~ (F & S) ⊃ L
2. (S & F) ⊃ L
3. (L v S) & (S ⊃ ~ F) — (~ L ⊃ S) & (S ⊃ ~ F)
4. ~ (L & F) v S
5. ~ [(L & F) v S]
6. ~ (L v F) & S

E. Some Tricky Translations
1. M — NOT: J & C
2. H — NOT: T ⊃ E
3. ~ A — NOT: ~ S
4. ~ S — NOT: ~ A

KEY for (E):
A = All of my friends are philosophers.
C = Cindy is married.
E = Hitler defeats England.
H = If Hitler had kept his treaty with Stalin, he would have defeated England.
J = Joe is married.
M = Joe and Cindy are married.
S = Some of my friends are philosophers.
T = Hitler keeps his treaty with Stalin.

8. Slowing down some Examples from 6D

NOTES

1. Unless Elmo is a liar, he is both a fool and a sexpot.

   L v (F & S)   ~ (F & S) ⊃ L

2. Both Elmo is a liar unless he is a sexpot and if he is a sexpot, he is not a fool.

   (L v S) & (S ⊃ ~ F)
   (~ L ⊃ S) & (S ⊃ ~ F)

3. Either it is not the case that Elmo is both a liar and a fool or Elmo is a sexpot.

   ______ v ______

   ______ v S

   … it is not the case that Elmo is both a liar and a fool …

   ~ (L & F) v S

CHAPTER 9

SL TRUTH-TABLES

A. Characteristic truth-table definitions:

P	$\sim P$	
T	F	[$\sim P$ is true iff P is false]
F	T	

P	Q	$P \& Q$	$P \vee Q$	$P \supset Q$	$P \equiv Q$
T	T	T	T	T	T
T	F	F	T	F	F
F	T	F	T	T	F
F	F	F	F	T	T

[$P \& Q$ is true iff both P and Q are true]
[$P \vee Q$ is false iff both P and Q are false]
[$P \supset Q$ is false iff P is true and Q is false]
[$P \equiv Q$ is true iff P and Q have the same truth-value]

B. Truth-table Tests:

1. Truth-functional Validity
2. Truth-functional Consistency
3. Truth-functional Equivalence
4. Truth-functional Truth, Falsity, and Indeterminacy

C. Three Things to Know:

NOTES

1. Characteristic Truth-table Definitions
2. How to Set-up Truth-tables
   Grammar of SL Sentences
3. How to Determine Whether a Property/Relation Holds

D. Truth-functional vs. Non-truth-functional Connectives

UNARY CONNECTIVES

P is false
∴, It is not the case that *P* is true

P is false
∴, It is possible that *P* is ???

For "*P*" = "All bachelors are women," the truth-value of the compound sentence is false but for "*P*" = "Joe is a woman," it is true. So, "it is possible that" is not a truth-functional connective.

BINARY CONNECTIVES

P is true and *Q* is true
∴, *P* and *Q* is true

P is true and *Q* is true
∴, *P* before *Q* is ???

Suppose that:

Locke was born	=	True
Leibniz was born	=	True

Is "Locke was born before Leibniz was born" true or false?
This cannot be determined from the information provided.
So, "before" is not a truth-functional connective.

E. Grammar of SL Sentences

1. Consider these four sentences:
   ~ [(A v B) ⊃ C]
   ~ (A v B) ⊃ C
   (~ A v B) ⊃ C
   ~ A v (B ⊃ C)

NOTES

2. The order for determining truth-values in truth-tables for the above sentences is described below: 0, 1, 2, 3. 0 is an optional step.

3 0 1 0 2 0	
~ [(A v B) ⊃ C]	Main connective is "~"
2 0 1 0 3 0	
~ (A v B) ⊃ C	Main connective is "⊃"
1 0 2 0 3 0	
(~ A v B) ⊃ C	Main connective is "⊃"
1 0 2 0 1 0	
~ A v (B ⊃ C)	Main connective is "v"

F. How to Determine Whether a Property/Relation Holds

For each property or relation, look at the truth-values under the *main connective* of each sentence.

1. T-F (truth-functional) Validity (two premises, one conclusion only)
   Look for: T-T-F
   If you find it: INVALID
   If you don't find it: VALID

2. T-F Consistency (three sentences only)
   Look for: T-T-T
   If you find it: CONSISTENT
   If you don't find it: INCONSISTENT

3. T-F Equivalence
   If they are the same on each row: EQUIVALENT
   If they differ on at least one row: NOT EQUIVALENT

4. T-F Truth, Falsity, and Indeterminacy
   If they are all T's: T-F TRUE
   If they are all F's: T-F FALSE
   If they are mixed (T's and F's): T-F INDETERMINATE

G. Understanding Definitions

Truth-functional Truth: A sentence *P* of SL is *truth-functionally true* (t-f true) iff *P* is true on every assignment of truth-values.

- Truth-value assignments correspond to rows so this means:
  P is t-f true iff there is a "T" under the main connective of *P* at every row in the truth-table.

Truth-functional Falsity: A sentence *P* of SL is *truth-functionally false* (t-f false) iff *P* is false on every assignment of truth-values.

NOTES

- Truth-value assignments correspond to rows so this means:
  P is t-f false iff there is an "F" under the main connective of *P* at every row in the truth-table.

Truth-functional Validity: An argument of SL is *truth-functionally valid* (t-f valid) iff there is no assignment of truth-values on which all the premises are true and the conclusion is false.

- Truth-value assignments correspond to rows so:
  An argument is t-f valid iff there is no row in which there is a "T" under the main connective of each of the premises and an "F" under the main connective of the conclusion.

Truth-functional Consistency: A theory of SL is *truth-functionally consistent* (t-f consistent) iff there is at least one assignment of truth-values on which all the sentences in the theory are true.

- Truth-value assignments correspond to rows so:
  A theory is t-f consistent iff there is a row in which there is a "T" under the main connective of each sentence in the theory.

H. Examples

1. Truth-functional truth, falsity, and indeterminacy
   $\sim P \vee P$
   $\sim (P \vee P)$
   $\sim (P \vee \sim P)$
   $\sim A \supset (B \supset \sim A)$
   $\sim (A \supset (B \supset A))$
   $\sim (A \supset B) \supset A$
   $(\sim A \supset B) \supset A$

2. Validity and invalidity
   I will pay you [Q] if you mow my lawn [P]. You mow my lawn, so I will pay you.
   $P \supset Q$
   $\underline{P}$
   Q

   I will pay you [P] only if you mow my lawn [Q]. You mow my lawn, so I will pay you.
   $P \supset Q$
   $\underline{Q}$
   P

NOTES

Other Examples:

$P \supset Q$	$P \supset Q$	$P \vee Q$	$P \vee Q$	$P \equiv Q$
$\sim P$	$\sim Q$	$\sim P$	P	$P \vee Q$
$\sim Q$	$\sim P$	Q	$\sim Q$	$P \& Q$

3. Consistency and inconsistency
   $\{P \supset Q, P, Q\}$
   $\{P \supset Q, P, \sim Q\}$
   $\{P \supset Q, \sim Q, \sim P\}$
   $\{P \vee Q, \sim P, Q\}$
   $\{P \vee Q, P, \sim Q\}$
   $\{P \equiv Q, P \vee Q, P \& Q\}$

4. Equivalence and non-equivalence

$\sim (P \vee \sim P)$	$P \& \sim P$	[logical falsity]
$\sim A \supset (B \supset \sim A)$	$B \supset B$	[logical truth]
$(\sim A \supset B) \supset A$	$B \supset A$	
$B \supset A$	$A \supset B$	['A if B' vs. 'A only if B']
$\sim (A \vee B)$	$\sim A \& \sim B$	[Neither A nor B]
$\sim (A \& B)$	$\sim A \& \sim B$	[Not both vs. both not]

<u>Here are some examples to work on but the answers are not in the text!</u>

$A \vee A$	A	
$A \& A$	A	
$\sim (A \vee B)$	$\sim A \vee \sim B$	
$\sim A \vee B$	$A \supset B$	[Not-A unless B]
$A \vee B$	$A \supset B$	
$A \supset B$	$\sim B \supset \sim A$	[sufficient and necessary conditions]

I. Answers to Truth-table Tests: Sentences

1. $\sim P \vee P$ — T-F TRUE

	1	0	↓	0
P	~	P	v	P
T	F	T	T	T
F	T	F	T	F

2. $\sim (P \vee P)$ — T-F INDETERMINATE

	↓	0	1	0
P	~	(P	v	P)
T	F	T	T	T
F	T	F	F	F

3. ~ (P v ~ P) T-F FALSE

	↓	0	2	1	0
P	~	(P	v	~	P)
T	F	T	T	F	T
F	F	F	T	T	F

4. ~ A ⊃ (B ⊃ ~ A) T-F TRUE

		1 0	↓	0	2	1 0
A	B	~ A	⊃	(B	⊃	~ A)
T	T	F	T	T	F	F
T	F	F	T	F	T	F
F	T	T	T	T	T	T
F	F	T	T	F	T	T

5. ~ (A ⊃ (B ⊃ A)) T-F FALSE

		↓	0	2	0	1	0
A	B	~	(A	⊃	(B	⊃	A))
T	T	F	T	T	T	T	T
T	F	F	T	T	F	T	T
F	T	F	F	T	T	F	F
F	F	F	F	T	F	T	F

6. ~ (A ⊃ B) ⊃ A T-F TRUE

		2	0	1	0	↓	0
A	B	~	(A	⊃	B)	⊃	A
T	T	F	T	T	T	T	T
T	F	T	T	F	F	T	T
F	T	F	F	T	T	T	F
F	F	F	F	T	F	T	F

7. (~ A ⊃ B) ⊃ A T-F INDETERMINATE

		1	0	2	0	↓	0
A	B	(~	A	⊃	B)	⊃	A
T	T	F		T	T	T	T
T	F	F		T	F	T	T
F	T	T		T	T	F	F
F	F	T		F	F	T	F

NOTES

NOTES

5. ~ (A ⊃ (B ⊃ A))

		↓	0		0		0
A	B	~	(A	⊃	(B	⊃	A))
T	T		T		T		T
T	F		T		F		T
F	T		F		T		F
F	F		F		F		F

6. ~ (A ⊃ B) ⊃ A

			0		0	↓	0
A	B	~	(A	⊃	B)	⊃	A
T	T		T		T		T
T	F		T		F		T
F	T		F		T		F
F	F		F		F		F

7. (~ A ⊃ B) ⊃ A

			0		0	↓	0
A	B	(~	A	⊃	B)	⊃	A
T	T				T		T
T	F				F		T
F	T				T		F
F	F				F		F

J. Properties of Sentences, in Slow Motion

5. ~ (A ⊃ (B ⊃ A))

		↓	0		0	1	0
A	B	~(	A	⊃	(B	⊃	A))
T	T		T		T	T	T
T	F		T		F	T	T
F	T		F		T	F	F
F	F		F		F	T	F

6. ~ (A ⊃ B) ⊃ A

			0	1	0	↓	0
A	B	~	(A	⊃	B)	⊃	A
T	T		T	T	T		T
T	F		T	F	F		T
F	T		F	T	T		F
F	F		F	T	F		F

NOTES

7. $(\sim A \supset B) \supset A$

		1	0		0	↓	0
A	B	(~	A	⊃	B)	⊃	A
T	T		F		T		T
T	F		F		F		T
F	T		T		T		F
F	F		T		F		F

5. $\sim (A \supset (B \supset A))$

		↓	0	2	0	1	0
A	B	~	(A	⊃	(B	⊃	A))
T	T		T	T	T	T	T
T	F		T	T	F	T	T
F	T		F	T	T	F	F
F	F		F	T	F	T	F

6. $\sim (A \supset B) \supset A$

		2	0	1	0	↓	0
A	B	~	(A	⊃	B)	⊃	A
T	T	F	T	T	T		T
T	F	T	T	F	F		T
F	T	F	F	T	T		F
F	F	F	F	T	F		F

7. $(\sim A \supset B) \supset A$

		1	0	2	0	↓	0
A	B	(~	A	⊃	B)	⊃	A
T	T	F		T	T		T
T	F	F		T	F		T
F	T	T		T	T		F
F	F	T		F	F		F

5. $\sim (A \supset (B \supset A))$

T-F FALSE

		↓	0	2	0	1	0
A	B	~	(A	⊃	(B	⊃	A))
T	T	F	T	T	T	T	T
T	F	F	T	T	F	T	T
F	T	F	F	T	T	F	F
F	F	F	F	T	F	T	F

NOTES

6. ~ (A ⊃ B) ⊃ A T-F TRUE

A	B	2 ~	0 (A	1 ⊃	0 B)	↓ ⊃	0 A
T	T	F	T	T	T	T	T
T	F	T	T	F	F	T	T
F	T	F	F	T	T	T	F
F	F	F	F	T	F	T	F

7. (~ A ⊃ B) ⊃ A T-F INDETERMINATE

A	B	1 (~	0 A	2 ⊃	0 B)	↓ ⊃	0 A
T	T	F		T	T	T	T
T	F	F		T	F	T	T
F	T	T		T	T	F	F
F	F	T		F	F	T	F

K. Answers to Truth-table Tests: Arguments

1. P ⊃ Q T-F VALID

P

———

Q

P	Q	P	↓ ⊃	Q	↓ P	↓ Q
T	T	T	T	T	T	T
T	F	T	F	F	T	F
F	T	F	T	T	F	T
F	F	F	T	F	F	F

2. P ⊃ Q T-F INVALID

Q

———

P

P	Q	P	↓ ⊃	Q	↓ Q	↓ P	
T	T	T	T	T	T	T	
T	F	T	F	F	F	T	
F	T	F	T	T	T	F	*
F	F	F	T	F	F	F	

NOTES

3. $P \supset Q$ / $\sim P$ / ∴ $\sim Q$ — T-F INVALID

P	Q	P	⊃ ↓	Q	~P ↓	~Q ↓	
T	T	T	T	T	F	F	
T	F	T	F	F	F	T	
F	T	F	T	T	T	F	*
F	F	F	T	F	T	T	

4. $P \supset Q$ / $\sim Q$ / ∴ $\sim P$ — T-F VALID

P	Q	P	⊃ ↓	Q	~Q ↓	~P ↓
T	T	T	T	T	F	F
T	F	T	F	F	T	F
F	T	F	T	T	F	T
F	F	F	T	F	T	T

5. $P \vee Q$ / $\sim P$ / ∴ Q — T-F VALID

P	Q	P	∨ ↓	Q	~P ↓	Q ↓
T	T	T	T	T	F	T
T	F	T	T	F	F	F
F	T	F	T	T	T	T
F	F	F	F	F	T	T

6. $P \vee Q$ / P / ∴ $\sim Q$ — T-F INVALID

P	Q	P	∨ ↓	Q	P ↓	~Q ↓	
T	T	T	T	T	T	F	*
T	F	T	T	F	T	T	
F	T	F	T	T	F	F	
F	F	F	F	F	F	T	

NOTES

7. P≡Q
P ∨ Q
———
P & Q

T-F VALID

P	Q	P	≡ ↓	Q	P	∨ ↓	Q	P	& ↓	Q
T	T	T	T	T	T	T	T	T	T	T
T	F	T	F	F	T	T	F	T	F	F
F	T	F	F	T	F	T	T	F	F	T
F	F	F	T	F	F	F	F	F	F	F

L. Answers to Truth-table Tests: Consistency

1. {P ⊃ Q, P, Q} T-F CONSISTENT

P	Q	0 P	↓ ⊃	0 Q	↓ P	↓ Q
T	T	T	T	T	T	T
T	F	T	F	F	T	F
F	T	F	T	T	F	T
F	F	F	T	F	F	F

2. {P ⊃ Q, P, ~ Q} T-F INCONSISTENT

P	Q	0 P	↓ ⊃	0 Q	↓ P	↓ 0 ~ Q
T	T	T	T	T	T	F
T	F	T	F	F	T	T
F	T	F	T	T	F	F
F	F	F	T	F	F	T

3. {P ⊃ Q, ~ Q, ~ P} T-F CONSISTENT

P	Q	0 P	↓ ⊃	0 Q	↓ ~ Q	↓ 0 ~ P
T	T	T	T	T	F	F
T	F	T	F	F	T	F
F	T	F	T	T	F	T
F	F	F	T	F	T	T

4. {P v Q, ~ P, Q}　　　T-F CONSISTENT

P	Q	P	v	Q	~ P	Q
		0	↓	0	↓	↓
T	T	T	T	T	F	T
T	F	T	T	F	F	F
F	T	F	T	T	T	T
F	F	F	F	F	T	F

5. {P v Q, P, ~ Q}　　　T-F CONSISTENT

P	Q	P	v	Q	P	~ Q
		0	↓	0	↓	↓ 0
T	T	T	T	T	T	F
T	F	T	T	F	T	T
F	T	F	T	T	F	F
F	F	F	F	F	F	T

6. {P ≡ Q, P v Q, P & Q}　　　T-F CONSISTENT

P	Q	P	≡	Q	P	v	Q	P	&	Q
		0	↓	0	0	↓	0	0	↓	0
T	T	T	T	T	T	T	T	T	T	T
T	F	T	F	F	T	T	F	T	F	F
F	T	F	F	T	F	T	T	F	F	T
F	F	F	T	F	F	F	F	F	F	F

7. {P ≡ Q, P v Q, ~ (P & Q)}　　　T-F INCONSISTENT

P	Q	P	≡	Q	P	v	Q	~	(P	&	Q)
		0	↓	0	0	↓	0	↓	0	1	0
T	T	T	T	T	T	T	T	F	T	T	T
T	F	T	F	F	T	T	F	T	T	F	F
F	T	F	F	T	F	T	T	T	F	F	T
F	F	F	T	F	F	F	F	T	F	F	F

NOTES

M. Answers to Truth-table Tests: Equivalence

1. ~(P ∨ ~P)
   P & ~P

	↓	0	2	1	0	0	↓	1	0
P	~	(*P*	∨	~	*P*)	*P*	&	~	*P*
T	F	T	T	F	T	T	F	F	
F	F	F	T	T	F	F	F	T	

T-F EQUIVALENT

2. ~A ⊃ (B ⊃ ~A)
   B ⊃ B

		1 0	↓	0	2	1 0	0	↓	0
A	B	~A	⊃	(B	⊃	~A)	B	⊃	B
T	T	F	T	T	F	F	T	T	T
T	F	F	T	F	T	F	F	T	F
F	T	T	T	T	T	T	T	T	T
F	F	T	T	F	T	T	F	T	F

T-F EQUIVALENT

3. (~A ⊃ B) ⊃ A
   B ⊃ A

		1 0	2	0	↓	0	0	↓	0
A	B	(~ A	⊃	B)	⊃	A	B	⊃	A
T	T	F	T	T	T	T	T	T	T
T	F	F	T	F	T	T	F	T	T
F	T	T	T	T	F	F	T	F	F
F	F	T	F	F	T	F	F	T	F

T-F EQUIVALENT

4. B ⊃ A
A ⊃ B

		0	↓	0	0	↓	0
A	B	B	⊃	A	A	⊃	B
T	T	T	T	T	T	T	T
T	F	F	T	T	T	F	F
F	T	T	F	F	F	T	T
F	F	F	T	F	F	T	F

NOT T-F EQUIVALENT

5. ~(A & B)
~A & ~B

		↓	0	1	0	1	0	↓	1	0
A	B	~	(A	&	B)	~	A	&	~	B
T	T	F	T	T	T		F	F		F
T	F	T	T	F	F		F	F		T
F	T	T	F	F	T		T	F		F
F	F	T	F	F	F		T	T		T

NOT T-F EQUIVALENT

6. ~(A v B)
~A & ~B

		↓	0	1	0	1	0	↓	1	0
A	B	~	(A	v	B)	~	A	&	~	B
T	T	F	T	T	T		F	F		F
T	F	F	T	T	F		F	F		T
F	T	F	F	T	T		T	F		F
F	F	T	F	F	F		T	T		T

T-F EQUIVALENT

NOTES

CHAPTER 10

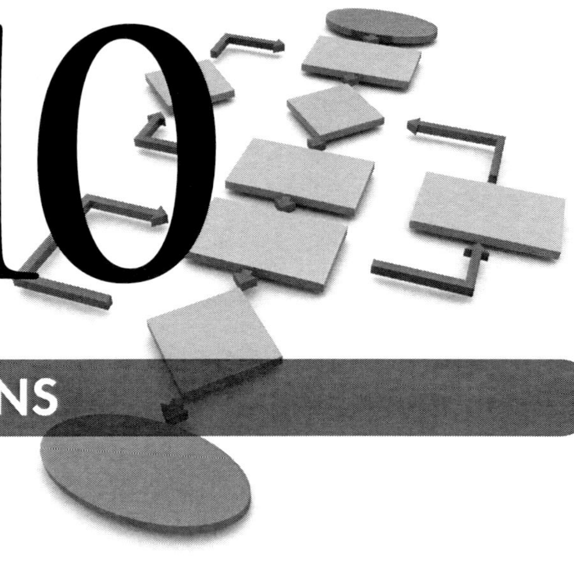

SL* AND SL+ DERIVATIONS

A. The Game of SL* (and SL+)

1. SL* is a game. The goal of the game is to perform derivations of SL sentences.
2. An SL* *derivation* is a sequence of SL sentences, subject to three restrictions.
   - The sentences in a derivation are *numerically ordered*, starting with the number 1.
   - The last sentence written is the sentence that is *derived*.
   - Each sentence in a derivation is *justified* by being either:
     (a) an *assumption*, or
     (b) a consequence of one of the 11 SL* rules and other previous sentence(s).

B. Some Facts About Games and SL* (and SL+)

1. Many games have rules that are essential to them. That is, if we do not follow those rules, then we are not really playing the game (or, at least we are not playing the game correctly). Think: Chess, Monopoly, etc.
   (a) In SL*, all of the rules are essential.
   (b) Therefore, to know how to play SL* is to know the rules. Primarily, it is to know how to use the SL* rules correctly.
2. The easiest way to understand a game (or the rules of a game) is to play the game.
3. The easiest way to get better at a game is to practice, that is, to play the game more often.

C. Ways of Playing SL* (and SL+)

NOTES

1. Top Down:
   Start with the sentences given as premises and try to derive the conclusion by manipulating symbols via the SL* rules.
   - You can only use this method with rules that you know!
   - Use this method for derivations in SL*.
2. Bottom Up:
   Use the algorithm below.
   - Use this method for derivations in SL* (unless you know the SL* rules really well).

RULES OF DERIVATION SYSTEM SL*

P, *Q*, etc. = any SL sentence
P, *Q*, etc. may be complex

R $\dfrac{P}{P}$

&I $\dfrac{\begin{array}{c}P\\ Q\end{array}}{P \,\&\, Q}$

Rule & I says: from sentences of the form *P* and *Q* derive a sentence of the form *P* & *Q*

&E $\dfrac{P \,\&\, Q}{P}$ or $\dfrac{P \,\&\, Q}{Q}$

∨I $\dfrac{P}{P \vee Q}$ or $\dfrac{P}{Q \vee P}$

∨E $P \vee Q$

| P
|———
| R

| Q
|———
| R

R

⊃I

| *P*
|———
| *Q*

$P \supset Q$

Rule ⊃ I says: If *Q* is derived from *P*, then derive $P \supset Q$

⊃E $\dfrac{\begin{array}{c}P \supset Q\\ P\end{array}}{Q}$

NOTES

≡I

| P
|---
| Q

| Q
|---
| P

$P \equiv Q$

≡E

$$\begin{array}{l} P \equiv Q \\ \underline{P} \\ Q \end{array} \quad \text{or} \quad \begin{array}{l} P \equiv Q \\ \underline{Q} \\ P \end{array}$$

RULES OF DERIVATION SYSTEM SL+: SL* RULES PLUS THE FOLLOWING:

1. Easy Rules

Com $\dfrac{P \& Q}{Q \& P}$ or $\dfrac{Q \& P}{P \& Q}$

$\dfrac{P \vee Q}{Q \vee P}$ or $\dfrac{Q \vee P}{P \vee Q}$

Assoc $\dfrac{P \& (Q \& R)}{(P \& Q) \& R}$ or $\dfrac{(P \& Q) \& R}{P \& (Q \& R)}$

$\dfrac{P \vee (Q \vee R)}{(P \vee Q) \vee R}$ or $\dfrac{(P \vee Q) \vee R}{P \vee (Q \vee R)}$

DN $\dfrac{P}{\sim\sim P}$ or $\dfrac{\sim\sim P}{P}$

2. Hard Rules

HS
$$\begin{array}{l} P \supset Q \\ \underline{Q \supset R} \\ P \supset R \end{array}$$

DS
$$\begin{array}{l} P \vee Q \\ \underline{\sim P} \\ Q \end{array}$$

MT
$$\begin{array}{l} P \supset Q \\ \underline{\sim Q} \\ \sim P \end{array}$$

Impl $\dfrac{P \supset Q}{\sim P \vee Q}$ or $\dfrac{\sim P \vee Q}{P \supset Q}$

DeM $\dfrac{\sim (P \vee Q)}{\sim P \& \sim Q}$ or $\dfrac{\sim P \& \sim Q}{\sim (P \vee Q)}$

$\dfrac{\sim (P \& Q)}{\sim P \vee \sim Q}$ or $\dfrac{\sim P \vee \sim Q}{\sim (P \& Q)}$

Trans $\dfrac{P \supset Q}{\sim Q \supset \sim P}$ or $\dfrac{\sim Q \supset \sim P}{P \supset Q}$

D. Examples: For each of the following, derive the required sentence in SL+.

NOTES

a. Derive: A

1.	(A & B) & C	Assumption

b. Derive: ~ ~ R

1.	P & (Q & R)	Assumption

c. Derive: R v Q

1.	P ≡ (Q v R)	Assumption
2.	P & Q	Assumption

NOTES

d. Derive: B ∨ C

1.	A ⊃ B	Assumption
2.	~ ~ A	Assumption

e. Derive: Q

1.	P ⊃ ~ ~ Q	Assumption
2.	~ ~ P	Assumption

f. Derive: L ∨ M

1.	~ (L & N) ≡ M	Assumption
2.	~ (L & N)	Assumption

g. Derive: ~ A

1.	$A \supset (B \& C)$	Assumption
2.	$\sim B$	Assumption

h. Derive: ~ (P & ~ Q)

1.	$P \supset Q$	Assumption

i. Derive: Q

1.	$P \& \sim P$	Assumption

NOTES

NOTES

E. Answers

a. Derive: A [Version 1]

1.	(A & B) & C	Assumption
2.	A & B	1 &E
3.	A	2 &E

a. Derive: A [Version 2]

1.	(A & B) & C	Assumption
2.	A & (B & C)	1 Assoc
3.	A	2 &E

b. Derive: ~ ~ R

1.	P & (Q & R)	Assumption
2.	(P & Q) & R	1 Assoc
3.	R	2 &E
4.	~ ~ R	3 DN

c. Derive: R ∨ Q

1.	P ≡ (Q ∨ R)	Assumption
2.	P & Q	Assumption
3.	Q	2 &E
4.	R ∨ Q	3 ∨I

d. Derive: B ∨ C

1.	A ⊃ B	Assumption
2.	~ ~ A	Assumption
3.	A	2 DN
4.	B	1, 3 ⊃E
5.	B ∨ C	4 ∨I

e. Derive: Q

1.	P ⊃ ~ ~ Q	Assumption
2.	~ ~ P	Assumption
3.	P	2 DN
4.	~ ~ Q	1, 3 ⊃E
5.	Q	4 DN

f. Derive: L v M

1.	~(L & N) ≡ M	Assumption
2.	~(L & N)	Assumption
3.	M	1, 2 ≡ E
4.	L v M	3 v E

g. Derive: ~A

1.	A ⊃ (B & C)	Assumption
2.	~B	Assumption
3.	~B v ~C	2 v I
4.	~(B & C)	3 DeM
5.	~A	1, 4 MT

h. Derive: ~ (P & ~ Q)

1.	P ⊃ Q	Assumption
2.	~P v Q	1 Impl
3.	~P v ~ ~Q	2 DN
4.	~(P& ~ Q)	3 DeM

i. Derive: Q

1.	P & ~ P	Assumption
2.	P	1 & E
3.	P v Q	2 v I
4.	~P	1 & E
5.	Q	3, 4 DS

NOTES

DERIVATIONS IN SL* (OR SL+)

A. Algorithm: Use whenever you want to determine how to derive a sentence, *P*, in SL*.

1. **Two-Step Version**

Step 1: Is *P* a component of some previous complex sentence, *Q*?
  YES: Use the appropriate elimination rule.
  NO: Go to step 2.

Step 2: Is *P* a complex sentence?
  YES: Use the appropriate introduction rule.
  NO: Try either v E or ~E. If this does not work, start over.

NOTES

2. **Three-Step Version**

Step 1. Is *P* a component of some previous complex sentence, *Q*?
YES: Is *Q* a conjunction, a conditional, a biconditional, or a disjunction?
YES: Try & E, ⊃ E, ≡ E or ∨ E.
NO: Go to Step 3.
NO: Go to Step 2.

Step 2. Is *P* a complex sentence?
YES: Is *P* a conjunction or a disjunction?
YES: Try & I or ∨ I.
NO: Is *P* a conditional or a biconditional?
YES: Try ⊃ I or ≡ I.
NO: Try ~ I.
NO: Go to Step 3.

Step 3. Is there a previous sentence, *Q*, which is a disjunction?
YES: Try ∨ E.
NO: Try ~ E. If this does not work, start over.

B. Derivations and Philosophical Arguments

1. The Problem of Evil: *Reductio ad Absurdum* [~ I, ~ E]
G = God exists
P = an all-powerful being exists
B = a benevolent being exists
K = an all-knowing being exists
E = evil exists

Derive: ~ G

1.	G ≡ [P & (B & K)]
2.	[P & (B & K)] ⊃ ~ E
3.	E

2. Socrates and Death: Constructive Dilemma [∨ E]
N = death is a state of nothingness
M = in death the soul migrates to another world
G = death is something good, not something bad

Derive: G

1.	N ∨ M
2.	N ⊃ G
3.	M ⊃ G

NOTES

3. The Problem of Free Will and Determinism: Conditional Proof [$\supset$ I]
   D = determinism is true
   A = people have alternative possibilities of action
   F = people have free will

   Derive: $D \supset \sim F$

1.	$D \supset \sim A$
2.	$F \supset A$

PART IV

PREDICATE LOGIC (PL)

CHAPTER 11

PREDICATE LOGIC TRANSLATIONS

THE LANGUAGE OF PREDICATE LOGIC (PL)

PL is an *extension* of SL.

PL includes SL symbols:

Sentence Letters:
A, B, C, …, A_1, B_1, etc.

Sentential Connectives:
~, &, ∨, ⊃, ≡

Punctuation Marks:
), (,], [

PL also includes other symbols not included in SL:

Variables:
w, x, y, z, …, w_1, etc.

Individual Constants:
a, b, c, …, a_1, etc.

Predicates (with Variables):
Ax, Bx, …, Axy, Bxy, …, Axyz, etc.

Quantifier Symbols:
∀, ∃ ⇒ (∀x), (∃x)

English Language Argument:

All women are mortal.

Madonna is a woman.

Madonna is mortal.

SL Translation:	PL Translation:
A	$(\forall x)(Wx \supset Mx)$
W	Wm
M	Mm

NOTES

EXAMPLES

A. No Quantifiers

KEY:

Bxyz: x is between y and z
Lxy: x loves y
Txy: x is taller than y
Hx: x is happy
Lx: x is a lawyer
Px: x is a philosopher
Rx: x is rich
Wx: x is a woman

a: Angelo
b: Barbara
c: Cindy
f: Florida
j: Joe
m: Maine
n: New York

1. Joe is a philosopher.
2. Joe and Angelo are philosophers.
3. Joe is taller than Angelo.
4. If Joe loves Cindy, then Angelo loves Barbara.
5. Barbara is either a philosopher or a lawyer.
6. Barbara is a happy philosopher.
7. If Cindy is a rich woman, then she is a woman.
8. Angelo loves Barbara but she does not love him.
9. New York is between Maine and Florida.

B. Quantifiers: Basic Categorical Sentences

KEY: **U.D.: everything**

Lx: x is a logician
Bx: x is beautiful
Fx: x is flawless
Hx: x is happy

Mx: x is a man
Px: x is a person
Wx: x is a woman

NOTES

1. All logicians are beautiful.
2. No logicians are flawless.
3. Some logicians are women.
4. Some logicians are not happy.
5. Everything is beautiful.
6. Nothing is flawless.
7. Something is happy.
8. Something is not beautiful.
9. Someone is not beautiful.
10. All flawless men are beautiful.
11. All men and women are beautiful.
12. Flawless women exist.
13. Flawless men are nonexistent.
14. Everything is either flawless or beautiful.
15. Everything is flawless or everything is beautiful.

C. Quantifiers: Restricted Universe of Discourse: Logicians

KEY:	**U.D.: logicians**	
	Bx: x is beautiful	Hx: x is happy
	Fx: x is flawless	Wx: x is a woman

1. All logicians are beautiful.
2. No logicians are flawless.
3. Some logicians are women.
4. Some logicians are not happy.

D. Quantifiers: Restricted Universe of Discourse: Persons

KEY:	**U.D.: persons**	
	Lxy: x likes y	Sx: x studies
	Txy: x is taller than y	m: Marvin
	Hx: x is happy	r: Rita
	Px: x will pass	s: Sue

1. Everyone is happy.
2. No one is happy.
3. Someone is happy.
4. Someone is unhappy.
5. Someone is taller than himself.
6. No one is taller than himself.
7. Someone is not taller than himself.
8. Someone likes Marvin.
9. Someone does not like Marvin.
10. No one likes Marvin.
11. Everyone likes Marvin.
12. Marvin likes everyone.

NOTES

13. Marvin likes someone.
14. Marvin does not like anyone.
15. Marvin does not like everyone.
16. Anyone who likes Sue likes Rita.
17. Everyone who likes Sue likes Rita.
18. If anyone likes Sue, Marvin does.
19. If everyone likes Sue, Marvin does.
20. If anyone likes Sue, he or she likes Rita.
21. If no one studies, no one will pass.
22. If everyone studies, everyone will pass.
23. If someone likes Sue, someone likes Rita.
24. If everyone likes Sue, everyone likes Rita.
25. Someone, but not everyone, likes Sue.
26. Someone likes Sue but someone does not.

E. Multiple Quantification

<u>KEY:</u> **U.D.: persons**
Lxy: x loves y

1. Someone loves someone.
2. Everyone loves everyone.
3. Someone loves everyone.
4. Everyone loves someone.
5. Someone is loved by someone.
6. Everyone is loved by everyone.
7. Someone is loved by everyone.
8. Everyone is loved by someone.

F. Harder Translations

<u>KEY:</u> **U.D.: everything**

Px: x is a person	Tx: x is a time
Lxy: x loves y	Lxyz: x loves y at z

1. Everyone is loved by someone.
2. Everybody loves somebody sometime.

NOTES

ANSWERS

A. No Quantifiers

KEY:	Bxyz: x is between y and z	
	Lxy: x loves y	a: Angelo
	Txy: x is taller than y	b: Barbara
	Hx: x is happy	d: Cindy
	Lx: x is a lawyer	f: Florida
	Px: x is a philosopher	j: Joe
	Rx: x is rich	m: Maine
	Wx: x is a woman	n: New York

1. Pj
2. Pj & Pa
3. Tja
4. Ljc ⊃ Lab
5. Pb v Lb
6. Hb & Pb
7. (Rc & Wc) ⊃ Wc
8. Lab & ~Lba
9. Bnmf

B. Quantifiers: Basic Categorical Sentences

KEY:	**U.D.: everything**	
	Lx: x is a logician	
	Bx: x is beautiful	Mx: x is a man
	Fx: x is flawless	Px: x is a person
	Hx: x is happy	Wx: x is a woman

1. (∀x)(Lx ⊃ Bx)		
2. (∀x)(Lx ⊃ ~Fx)		
3. (∃x)(Lx & Wx)		
4. (∃x)(Lx & ~Hx)		
5. (∀x)Bx		
6. (∀x) ~Fx	or	~(∃x)Fx
7. (∃x)Hx		
8. (∃x) ~Bx	or	~(∀x)Fx
9. (∃x)(Px & ~Bx)		
10. (∀x)((Fx & Mx) ⊃ Bx)		
11. (∀x)((Mx v Wx) ⊃ Bx)	or	(∀x)(Mx ⊃ Bx) & (∀x)(Wx ⊃ Bx)
12. (∃x)(Fx & Wx)		
13. ~(∃x)(Fx & Mx)	or	(∀x) ~(Fx & Mx)
	or	(∀x)(Fx ⊃ ~Mx)
	or	(∀x)(Mx ⊃ ~Fx)
14. (∀x) (Fx v Bx)		
15. (∀x)Fx v (∀x)Bx		

C. Quantifiers: Restricted Universe of Discourse: Logicians

NOTES

KEY:	**U.D.: logicians**	
	Bx: x is beautiful	Hx: x is happy
	Fx: x is flawless	Wx: x is a woman

1. (∀x)Bx
2. (∀x) ~Fx or ~(∃x)Fx
3. (∃x)Wx
4. (∃x) ~H x or ~(∀x)Hx

D. Quantifiers: Restricted Universe of Discourse: Persons

KEY:	**U.D.: persons**	
	Lxy: x likes y	Sx: x studies
	Txy: x is taller than y	m: Marvin
	Hx: x is happy	r: Rita
	Px: x will pass	s: Sue

1. (∀x)Hx
2. (∀x) ~Hx or ~(∃x)Hx
3. (∃x)Hx
4. (∃x) ~Hx or ~(∀x)Hx
5. (∃x)Txx
6. (∀x) ~Txx or ~(∃x)Txx
7. (∃x) ~Txx or ~(∀x)Txx
8. (∃x)Lxm
9. (∃x)~Lxm or ~(∀x)Lxm
10. (∀x) ~Lxm or ~(∃x)Lxm
11. (∀x)Lxm
12. (∀x)Lmx
13. (∃x)Lmx
14. ~(∃x)Lmx or (∀x) ~Lmx
15. ~(∀x)Lmx or (∃x) ~Lmx
16. (∀x)(Lxs ⊃ Lxr)
17. (∀x)(Lxs ⊃ Lxr)
18. (∃x)Lxs ⊃ Lms or (∀x)(Lxs ⊃ Lms)
19. (∀x)Lxs ⊃ Lms or (∃x)(Lxs ⊃ Lms)
20. (∀x)(Lxs ⊃ Lxr)
21. (∀x) ~Sx ⊃ (∀x) ~Px or ~(∃x)Sx ⊃ ~(∃x)Px
22. (∀x)Sx ⊃ (∀x)Px
23. (∃x)Lxs ⊃ ($x)Lxr
24. (∀x)Lxs ⊃ (∀x)Lxr
25. (∃x)Lxs & ~(∀x)Lxs or (∃x)Lxs & (∃x) ~Lxs
26. (∃x)Lxs & (∃x)~Lxs or (∃x)Lxs & ~(∀x)Lxs

NOTES

E. Multiple Quantification

<u>KEY:</u> **U.D.: persons**
Lxy: x loves y

1. $(\exists x)(\exists y)Lxy$
2. $(\forall x)(\forall y)Lxy$
3. $(\exists x)(\forall y)Lxy$
4. $(\forall x)(\exists y)Lxy$
5. $(\exists x)(\exists y)Lyx$
6. $(\forall x)(\forall y)Lyx$
7. $(\exists x)(\forall y)Lyx$
8. $(\forall x)(\exists y)Lyx$

PL TRANSLATION RULES

1. The order of quantity terms ("any," "every," "someone," "nothing," etc.) and negations should always be preserved in your PL translations.

2. Generally, the number of quantity terms equals the number of PL quantifiers. (Exception: "All men and women are beautiful.")

3. Generally, the main binary connective within the scope of an existential quantifier is an ampersand, "&." (Possible exception: "If everyone likes Sue, Marvin does.")

4. Generally, the main binary connective within the scope of a universal quantifier is a horseshoe, "$\supset$." (Possible exception: "Flawless men are nonexistent.")

5. Generally, if a sentence starts with a quantity term, the quantifier will have wide scope, that is, the quantifier will be the main operator. (Exceptions: "Everything is flawless or everything is beautiful," "Someone, but not everyone, likes Sue," etc.)

6. Generally, if a sentence starts with an "if," it is a conditional and the horseshoe, "$\supset$," will be the main operator. Thus, the quantifier will not have wide scope. (Exceptions: "If anyone likes Sue, he or she likes Rita;" "If anyone likes Sue, Marvin does.")

7. Generally, "anything" means "everything" unless it follows "not" or "if" (which is a special case of "not"). (Possible exception: "If anyone likes Sue, he or she likes Rita.")

CHAPTER 12

DERIVATION RULES

1. Scope Rules (SR):

$(\forall x)\ Px \vee Pa$	=	$(\forall x)\ (Px \vee Pa)$
$(\forall x)\ Px \,\&\, Pa$	=	$(\forall x)\ (Px \,\&\, Pa)$
$(\exists x)\ Px \vee Pa$	=	$(\exists x)\ (Px \vee Pa)$
$(\exists x)\ Px \,\&\, Pa$	=	$(\exists x)\ (Px \,\&\, Pa)$

   Above "*P*x" is a PL expression with variable "x" and "*P*a" is a PL sentence with no variables.

2. Quantifier Negation (QN):

$\sim(\exists x)P$	=	$(\forall x) \sim P$
$\sim(\forall x)P$	=	$(\exists x) \sim P$

3. Any SL+ Derivation Rule

EXAMPLES OF PD* DERIVATIONS

I.	1.	$(\forall x)(Sx \supset Px)$	Assumption	[A-type sentence]
	2.	$(\forall x)(\sim Sx \vee Px)$	1 Impl	
	3.	$(\forall x)(\sim Sx \vee \sim \sim Px)$	2 DN	
	4.	$(\forall x) \sim(Sx \,\&\, \sim Px)$	3 DeM	
	5.	$\sim(\exists x)(Sx \,\&\, \sim Px)$	4 QN	[negated O-type sentence]

II.	1.	$(\forall x)(Sx \supset \sim Px)$	Assumption	[E-type sentence]
	2.	$(\forall x)(\sim Sx \vee \sim Px)$	1 Impl	
	3.	$(\forall x) \sim(Sx \,\&\, Px)$	2 DeM	
	4.	$\sim(\exists x)(Sx \,\&\, Px)$	3 QN	[negated I-type sentence]

III. 1.	$(\exists x)(Sx \,\&\, Px)$	Assumption	[I-type sentence]
2.	$(\exists x)(\sim\sim Sx \,\&\, Px)$	1 DN	
3.	$(\exists x)\sim(\sim Sx \vee \sim Px)$	2 DeM	
4.	$(\exists x)\sim(Sx \supset \sim Px)$	3 Impl	
5.	$\sim(\forall x)(Sx \supset \sim Px)$	4 QN	[negated E-type sentence]
IV. 1.	$(\exists x)(Sx \,\&\, \sim Px)$	Assumption	[O-type sentence]
2.	$(\exists x)(\sim\sim Sx \,\&\, \sim Px)$	1 DN	
3.	$(\exists x)\sim(\sim Sx \vee Px)$	2 DeM	
4.	$(\exists x)\sim(Sx \supset Px)$	3 Impl	
5.	$\sim(\forall x)(Sx \supset Px)$	4 QN	[negated A-type sentence]
V. 1.	$(\exists x)Lxs \supset Lms$	Assumption	[If anyone loves Sally, ...]
2.	$\sim(\exists x)Lxs \vee Lms$	1 Impl	
3.	$(\forall x)\sim Lxs \vee Lms$	2 QN	
4.	$(\forall x)(\sim Lxs \vee Lms)$	3 SR	
5.	$(\forall x)(Lxs \supset Lms)$	4 Impl	
VI. 1.	$(\forall x)Lxs \supset Lms$	Assumption	[If everyone loves Sally, ...]
2.	$\sim(\forall x)Lxs \vee Lms$	1 Impl	
3.	$(\exists x)\sim Lxs \vee Lms$	2 QN	
4.	$(\exists x)(\sim Lxs \vee Lms)$	3 SR	
5.	$(\exists x)(Lxs \supset Lms)$	4 Impl	

Note: All of these derivations utilize *equivalence rules* only, so one can reverse the proofs and derive the first sentence from the last one in each case. For instance, in both (V) and (VI) you can derive (1) from (5) by using these rules in this order: Assumption, Impl, SR, QN, and Impl. In addition, for each derivation, the initial assumption is equivalent to each and every sentence that is derived from it.

NOTES

Highlight of Judge Conner's decision on Ohio soft drink tax:

- Judge declares that soft drinks are food.

  "...it is common knowledge that soft drinks are a staple in almost everyone's diet. Society's reliance of soft drinks is further evidenced by the number of vending machines and other sources offering them for sale."

  "...it is better we should look to the definitions of food when the legislature is defining it for the total benefit of the public welfare and not to satisfy the sometimes insatiable appetite of government to levy, raise, and collect taxes."

  "...the court finds the word food as it is used in Art. XII, Sec. 3(c) of the Ohio Constitution includes soft drinks."

- Constitutional prohibition against taxing food allows food to be taxed at wholesale level.

  "A reading of the plain language of the amendment dictates that not all sales of food are to be tax exempt."

  "The tax at issue herein is imposed at the wholesale level. Although a retailer may ultimately be charged with the payment of the tax, it still remains a tax on the sale between the wholesaler and retailer."

CONCLUSION:

If soft drinks are legally defined as food and they can be taxed at the wholesale level, any food product can be taxed at the wholesale level.

STOP THE TAX

1·800·XXX.XXXX

LOGICAL ANALYSIS OF "STOP THE TAX"

NOTES

A. Argument as Presented

1. Judge declares that soft drinks are food.
2. Constitution prohibition against taxing food allows food to be taxed at wholesale level.
   a. A reading of the plain language of the amendment dictates that not all sales of food are to be tax exempt.
   b. The tax at issue here is on the wholesale level.

Conclusion: If soft drinks are legally defined as food and they can be taxed at the wholesale level, any food product can be taxed at the wholesale level.

B. Reconstruction of Argument

1. Soft drinks are legally defined as food.
2. <u>Soft drinks can be taxed at the wholesale level.</u>
3. Any food product can be taxed at the wholesale level.

C. Alternative Conclusion

1. Not all foods are tax exempt.

D. Symbolization Key

Sx: x is a soft drink
Fx: x is a food
Tx: x can be taxed [= ~Ex]
Ex: x is tax exempt [= ~Tx]

E. Predicate Logic Translations

1. Soft drinks are legally defined as food.
   = Some soft drinks are food = $(\exists x)\ (Sx\ \&\ Fx)$

2. Soft drinks can be taxed at the wholesale level.
   = All soft drinks can be taxed = $(\forall x)\ (Sx \supset Tx)$

3. Any food product can be taxed at the wholesale level.
   = Any food can be taxed = $(\forall x)\ (Fx \supset Tx)$
   = No foods are tax exempt = $(\forall x)\ (Fx \supset {\sim}Ex)$

NOTES

4. Not all sales of food are to be tax exempt.
   = Not all foods are tax exempt = (a) = $\sim(\forall x)(Fx \supset Ex)$
   = It is not the case that no foods can be taxed = $\sim(\forall x)(Fx \supset \sim Tx)$
   = Some foods are not tax exempt = (b) = $(\exists x)(Fx \,\&\, \sim Ex)$
   = Some foods can be taxed = $(\exists x)(Fx \,\&\, Tx)$

F. Derivation of (b) from (a) [works from (b) to (a), as well] (See Ch. 19, sec. B, no. IV)

1.	$\sim(\forall x)(Fx \supset Ex)$	Assumption
2.	$(\exists x) \sim(Fx \supset Ex)$	1 QN
3.	$(\exists x) \sim(\sim Fx \vee Ex)$	2 Impl
4.	$(\exists x)(\sim \sim Fx \,\&\, \sim Ex)$	3 DeM
5.	$(\exists x)(Fx \,\&\, \sim Ex)$	4 DN

G. Conclusions

Not all foods are tax exempt = Some foods are not tax exempt
Any food can be taxed = No foods are tax exempt
No foods are tax exempt ≠ Not all foods are tax exempt
Not all foods are tax exempt ≠ Any food can be taxed

PART V

FALLACIES

Definitions: We reason **fallaciously** whenever we reason from an argument that (1) is invalid or weak, (2) has premises that are either false or unwarranted, or (3) is missing relevant information. A **fallacy** is an argument that is deficient in one of these ways yet is also psychologically persuasive.

NOTES

Formal Fallacies (Chapter 13)

A. SL Fallacies
   1. Affirming the Consequent
   2. Denying the Antecedent
   3. Affirming the Disjunct
   4. Converting the Components
   5. Negating the Components
   6. Distribution Fallacies

B. PL Fallacies
   1. Scope Fallacies
   2. Name Fallacies

Inductive Fallacies (Chapter 14)

A. General Inductive Fallacies
   1. Questionable Statistics
   2. Small Sample
   3. Unrepresentative Sample
   4. Suppressed Evidence

B. Fallacies of Causation
   1. Questionable Cause
   2. Causal Slippery Slope

Informal Fallacies (Chapter 15)

A. Problematic Premise Fallacies
   1. Begging the Question
   2. False Dilemma

B. Linguistic Fallacies
   1. Equivocation
   2. Vagueness

C. Part/Whole Fallacies
   1. Composition
   2. Division

D. Fallacies of Diversion
   1. Ad Hominem
   2. Appeal to Ignorance
   3. Appeal to Pity
   4. Appeal to Force

E. Inadequate Appeals
   1. Appeal to Authority
   2. Appeal to Popularity
   3. Two Wrongs Make a Right
   4. Appeal to Common Practice

CHAPTER 13

FORMAL FALLACIES

PART A: SL FALLACIES

A lot of arguments seem good because they are similar in certain respects to arguments that are good. Below are six fallacies that are all similar to valid inference rules in SD+.

1. **Fallacy: Affirming the Consequent**

   $P \supset Q$
   $\underline{Q}$
   P

   Valid Argument Form: Modus Ponens ($\supset$ E)

   $P \supset Q$
   $\underline{P}$
   Q

   Example of Fallacy: Jan is a person if Jan is a woman. Jan is a person, so Jan is a woman.

2, **Fallacy: Denying the Antecedent**

   $P \supset Q$
   $\underline{\sim P}$
   $\sim Q$

   Valid Argument Form: Modus Tollens (MT)

   $P \supset Q$
   $\underline{\sim Q}$
   $\mathbf{\sim P}$

Example of Fallacy: Carl embezzled the college funds only if he is guilty of a felony. Carl did not embezzle the college funds, so Carl is not guilty of a felony.

NOTES

3. **Fallacy: Affirming the Disjunct**

$$\frac{\begin{array}{l} P \vee Q \\ P \end{array}}{\sim Q}$$

Valid Argument Form: Disjunctive Syllogism (DS)

$$\frac{\begin{array}{l} P \vee Q \\ \sim P \end{array}}{Q}$$

Example of Fallacy: Either your dog has run away from home or a car has hit her. Your dog has run away from home, so a car has not hit her.

4. **Fallacy: Converting the Components**

$P \supset Q \neq Q \supset P$

Valid Argument Form: Transposition (Trans)

$P \supset Q = \sim Q \supset \sim P$

Example of Fallacy: The streets are wet if it is raining, so it is raining if the streets are wet.

5. **Fallacy: Negating the Components**

$P \supset Q \neq \sim P \supset \sim Q$

Valid Argument Form: Transposition (Trans)

$P \supset Q = \sim Q \supset \sim P$

Example of Fallacy: The streets are wet if it is raining, so the streets are not wet if it is not raining.

6. **Fallacy: Distribution Fallacies**

(a) $\sim P \vee \sim Q \sim \neq \sim(P \vee Q)$
(b) $\sim(P \,\&\, Q) \neq \sim P \,\&\, \sim Q$

Valid Argument Form: DeMorgan (DeM)

$\sim(P \vee Q) = \sim P \,\&\, \sim Q$
$\sim(P \,\&\, Q) = \sim P \vee \sim Q$

Example of Fallacy (a): Joe is either not a Democrat or not a Republican. Therefore, Joe is neither a Democrat nor a Republican.

Example of Fallacy (b): It is not the case that Joe is both a Democrat and a Republican, so Joe is both not a Democrat and not a Republican.

NOTES

PART B: PL FALLACIES

1. There is a head and John does not have it. Therefore, John does not have a head.

   This argument is translated in PL as follows:
   $(\exists x)$ (Hx & ~Hjx)
   ∴, ~$(\exists x)$ (Hx & Hjx)

   The argument is an example of a **scope fallacy** since the negation changes from **narrow scope** (in the premise) to **wide scope** (in the conclusion). Given the rule QN noted above (Ch. 16), a negated existential sentence is equivalent to a universal sentence. One cannot derive a universal sentence from an existential sentence, so the above argument is invalid.

2. No one is taller than Jim and Jim is taller than Alan. Therefore, no one is taller than Alan.

   This argument is translated in PL as follows:
   ~$(\exists x)$ Txj = $(\forall x)$ ~Txj
   Tja
   ∴, ~$(\exists x)$ Txa = $(\forall x)$ ~Txa

   This is an example of a **name fallacy** since it treats the expression "no one" as if it were a name designating a person, like "Barry." For instance, the following argument is valid:

   Barry is taller than Jim and Jim is taller than Alan. Thus, Barry is taller than Alan.

   The logic of quantity terms, like "no one," is much more complex than the logic of names. As it turns out, (2) is invalid since if Jim is taller than Alan, the conclusion must be false.

3. If someone is in Pullman, then he is not in Moscow. A man is in Pullman. Therefore, there is not a man in Moscow.

   This argument is translated in PL as follows:
   $(\forall x)(Px \supset \sim Mx)$
   $(\exists x)Px$
   ∴, ~$(\exists x)Mx$

   This is an example of a **name fallacy** since the following argument is valid:
   $(\forall x)(Px \supset \sim Mx)$
   Pb
   ∴, ~Mb

   Again, the logic of quantity terms like "someone" is much more complex than the logic of names. The conclusion of this argument is false even though the premises are true.

4. Everyone is loved by someone. Therefore, there is someone who loves everyone.

   This argument is translated in PL as follows:

$(\forall x)(\exists y)Lyx$	=	$(\forall y)(\exists x)Lxy$
$\therefore$, $(\exists y)(\forall x)Lyx$	=	$(\exists x)(\forall y)Lxy$

   [Note that usually when we translate quantity sentences, we begin with the variable "x." But in order to see how the premise and conclusion are logically related, it is best to keep the order of variables the same in the predicates.]

   This is an example of a **scope fallacy**. In the premise, the universal quantifier has wide scope but in the conclusion, the existential quantifier has wide scope. The premise is not equivalent to the conclusion. The former is consistent with the claim that each particular person is loved by a different person but the latter is not.

5. Not all foods are tax exempt. Therefore, any food product can be taxed.

   This argument is translated in PL as follows:
   $\sim(\forall x)(Fx \supset Ex)$
   $\therefore$, $(\forall x)(Fx \supset \sim Ex)$

   [Note that "any food product can be taxed" just means "no food product is tax exempt." This allows us to translate the conclusion with the same predicates as the premise.]

   This is an example of a **scope fallacy** since the negation changes from wide scope (in the premise) to narrow scope (in the conclusion). Given the rule QN noted above, a negated universal sentence is equivalent to an existential sentence. One cannot derive a universal sentence from an existential sentence, so the above argument is invalid.

6. Someone is not a woman, so it is not the case that someone is a woman.

   This argument is translated in PL as follows:
   $(\exists x) \sim Wx$
   $\therefore$, $\sim(\exists x) Wx$

   This is an example of a **scope fallacy** since the existential quantifier and the negation change scope. Given QN, when this happens, the quantifier needs to change as well.

7. Someone is rich, so someone is not rich.

   This argument is translated in PL as follows:
   $(\exists x) Rx$
   $\therefore$, $\sim(\exists x) Rx$

   The argument is invalid. Conversational implicature is distinct from implication.

CHAPTER 14

INDUCTIVE FALLACIES

The premises of any cogent inductive argument provide good, but not conclusive, grounds for accepting the conclusion. This evidential "gap" between the premises and conclusion is not entirely bad. For any valid deductive argument, the information content of the conclusion is already contained in the premises but in a cogent inductive argument, the content of the conclusion always exceeds that of the premises. This allows us to expand our knowledge: to reason from past facts to future predictions, or to derive theories from mere observations.

A. Types of Inductive Arguments:

1. **Generalization**: All observed swans are white, so all swans are white.
2. **Statistical Induction**: 95% of observed swans are white, so most swans are white.
3. **Argument from Analogy**: Objects *a* and *b* are *F*, *G*, etc. (i.e., they have properties *F*, *G*, etc. in common); *a* is H, as well. Therefore, *b* is H.
4. **Causal Argument**: an inductive argument with a **causal claim** in the conclusion.

B. Polls

Facts about sample size:

1. Greater sample size yields higher probability.
2. More representative samples yield higher probability.
3. One definite counterexample invalidates any complete generalization.

Unreliable Surveys:

1. Person-on-the-street polls
2. Self-selecting-sample polls (1-900 polls, mail-in polls)

C. Bayes's Theorem

NOTES

Suppose Bob tests positive for drug-use at work. Suppose also that:

- the drug test is 90% accurate;
- 10% of the workers use drugs.

What is the probability that Bob actually uses drugs? Answer: 50%

Explanation: Suppose that there are 1,000 workers and all of them are tested for drug use.
900 workers would be non-drug users
90% of them would test negative = 810
10% of them would test positive = 90 (These are *false positives.*)
100 workers would be drug users
90% of them would test positive = 90 (These are *true positives.*)
10% of them would test negative = 10

The number of true positives equals the number of false positives. Thus, of those who test positive, only half are drug users!

D. General Inductive Fallacies

1. **Questionable Statistics** =df. the misuse of statistics in an argument.
   Example: He failed the drug test. The drug test is 90% accurate so he probably uses drugs. (See Bayes's Theorem, above.)

2. **Small Sample** =df. basing a conclusion on a sample size that is too small to be a reliable measure of the population.
   Example: My first wife wouldn't let me watch sports on TV and neither would my second wife. Don't get married because women hate sports on TV.

3. **Unrepresentative Sample** =df. basing a conclusion on a sample size that is not representative of the population as a whole.
   Example: 87% of Rush Limbaugh's audience is in favor of the new tax raise. Therefore, most Americans are in favor of it.

4. **Suppressed Evidence** =df. presenting an inductive argument that is missing *relevant information.*
   Example: Most coffee drinkers develop heart disease. Therefore, we can conclude that drinking coffee is bad for your heart.

   More specifically, the missing information is such that, if it were included in the original argument, it would substantially weaken the inference of the premises to the conclusion. Hence, this is *not merely a fallacy about missing information.*

NOTES

E. Fallacies of Causation

1. **Questionable Cause** =df. a weak causal argument [A **causal argument** is an argument with a causal claim as a conclusion. A **causal claim** is a claim that suggests some causal relation: *X* happens (e.g., pain relief) because *Y* happens (e.g., chiropractic treatment).]
   Example: 90% of those who undergo chiropractic treatment are relieved of their lower back pain within a week. Therefore, chiropractic care is effective for treatment of lower back pain.

   Four cells of information:
   a. How many people were cured after treatment?
   b. How many people were not cured after treatment?
   c. How many people were cured without treatment?
   d. How many people were not cured without treatment?

   Types of Questionable Cause:
   a. Confusing correlation with causation.
   b. Disregarding negative co-relations.
   c. Ignoring common causes.

2. **Causal Slippery Slope** =df. wrongfully arguing against a certain action based on the assumption that once the action is taken a chain of events will result that eventually leads to a catastrophe. Given that the assumption is either false or left unsupported, the argument is fallacious.
   Example: If we don't do something about Nicaragua, then sooner or later it will fall to communism. And then El Salvador will fall, and then Mexico will fall, and before long we'll be passing out Mao's little red book on the street corners in Brownsville, Texas.

CHAPTER 15

INFORMAL FALLACIES

A. Problematic Premise Fallacies

1. **Begging the Question** =df. the conclusion is a restatement of one of the premises.

   Example A: Whether or not a woman carries a baby to term is her decision and hers only since she is the only person directly involved.

   Example B: Abortion is murder, plain and simple. For it is the unjustified killing of an innocent person.

2. **False Dilemma** =df. a premise of the argument suggests that there are only two alternatives when, in fact, there are more than two alternatives. Sometimes the dilemma is *suppressed*.

   Example: Either we make use of the death penalty or we set murderers free and allow them to go on killing innocent people. But no one thinks that innocent people should die so we must make use of the death penalty.

B. Linguistic Fallacies

Ambiguity vs. Vagueness

- A word is **ambiguous** if it has two different meanings
  Bank: area near river vs. financial institution
- A word is **vague** if there is a "grey area" where it is unclear whether or not the term applies
  Bald: How much hair needs to be missing in order for someone to count as being bald?

1. **Equivocation** =df. an argument that is invalid due to the ambiguity of one or more words. More specifically, there is at least one word used in the argument with two different meanings and, given the two meanings, the argument is invalid. In addition, if we were to hold the meaning fixed, then one of the premises of the argument would be false.

   Example: Radicals should be banned from campus and some numbers are radical, so some numbers should be banned from campus.

2. **Vagueness** =df. an invalid inference that exploits the vagueness of at least one of the words in the argument.

   Example: There's no clear biological difference between men and women, so there is no such thing as human sexuality.

C. Part/Whole Fallacies

1. **Composition** (a.k.a., the salesman's fallacy) =df. reasoning that something has a property based on the fact that its parts have that property. [Parts to whole.]

   Example: Each monthly payment is cheap, so the car is cheap.

2. **Division** =df. reasoning that the parts of something have a property based on the fact that the whole thing has that property. [Whole to parts.]

   Example: The rooms of a large hotel must be large since the hotel is large.

D. Fallacies of Diversion

1. **Ad Hominem** =df. an irrelevant personal attack [*ad hominem* =df. to the person or man].

   Example A: Bill Clinton was not a good President for he committed adultery.

   Example B: Frank Sinatra is a gangster since all of his friends are gangsters.

   Types of Ad Hominem Arguments:
   A. **Abusive ad hominem**: An irrelevant attack on a person rather than her argument.
   B. **Circumstantial ad hominem**: Guilt by association.

2. **Appeal to Ignorance** =df. arguing that a claim is true based merely on the assumption that has not proven to be false.

   Example: God certainly exists because every attempt to prove that He does not exist has failed.

3. **Appeal to Pity** =df. attempting to persuade one of a conclusion by merely appealing to the sentiment of pity.

   Example: Give money to philosophers because otherwise they will starve to death.

4. **Appeal to Force** =df. attempting to persuade one of a conclusion by merely appealing to the unfortunate consequences that might come to those who fail to believe.

   Example: Believe that God exists, for if you don't, you'll spend an eternity in Hell!

E. Inadequate Appeals

1. **Appeal to Authority** =df. attempting to justify a **belief** by appeal to an alleged expert. Though the person may be an expert in some field, he is not an expert on the subject of discussion.

   Example: Wheaties must be good because Michael Jordan says that they are.

2. **Appeal to Popularity** =df. attempting to justify a **belief** by appealing to the fact that **lots of people believe it** or have believed it.

   Example: In every culture people accept that God exists. Thus, She does exist.

3. **Two Wrongs Make a Right** =df. attempting to justify an **action** done to some person (or group) by appealing to the fact that he (or they) did the same thing.

   Example: It's okay to torture terrorists since they torture us.

4. **Appeal to Common Practice** =df. attempting to justify an **action** by appealing to the fact that **lots of people do it** or have done it.

   Example: Everyone speeds on the highway. Hence, it is okay for me to speed on the highway.

Commonly Asked Questions:

How does Appeal to Popularity differ from Appeal to Common Practice?

- Popularity attempts to justify a *belief* based on the fact that many hold the belief.
- Common Practice attempts to justify an *action* based on the fact that many do it.

How does Two Wrongs Make a Right differ from Appeal to Common Practice?

- Two Wrongs attempts to justify an action toward *X* based on the fact that *X* did it, where *X* is an *individual* person or group.

- Common Practice attempts to justify an action based on the fact that *many* do it.

NOTES

Examples of Informal Fallacies

1. The end of a thing is its purpose and death is the end of life, so death is the purpose of life.
2. Fetal-tissue experimentation is wrong because it will lead to planned abortions and the harvesting of fetuses.
3. I can eat meat because most other people do.
4. I would never vote for Nixon since the KKK supported him.
5. Most people who take heroin started out on marijuana, so marijuana use leads to heroin use.
6. According to Christian belief, abortion is wrong. Thus, abortion must be wrong since most American's are Christian.
7. We should reject Michael Jordan's view on affirmative action for he is just a basketball player.
8. Over the past 30 years—a period when American women began using the pill regularly—life expectancy *increased* significantly among these women. Therefore, the pill is not a major health threat.
9. God is love; love is blind; Ray Charles is blind. Therefore, Ray Charles is God.
10. It's okay to torture Arab terrorists since they often torture Americans.
11. Whether or not a woman carries a baby to term is her decision and her decision only for she is the only person directly involved.
12. Albert Einstein believed in the existence of all-powerful God. Hence, such a God must exist.
13. If we allow first-trimester abortion, then soon we'll allow late-term abortion and eventually the country will be rampant in infanticide.
14. Pornography shouldn't be illegal because there's no way to draw a line between pornography and eroticism.
15. Over half of the prison population has had at least one homosexual experience. We can therefore conclude that at least half of all men are homosexuals.
16. America is the richest country in the world. You are an American, so you must be very rich.
17. The earth is flat for everyone believes that it is flat.
18. All of my friends are voting for Clinton. Hence, Clinton should win.
19. This stereo is cheap because 50 dollars is not a lot of money, and you can have this stereo for just 50 dollars a week.
20. Frank Sinatra is corrupt since most of his friends are gangsters.
21. The war on drugs is not working, so we must legalize all drugs.
22. No one can prove that God does not exist. Hence, it is reasonable to conclude that He does.
23. My mom wouldn't let me go to the movies this afternoon, and she won't let me stay up and watch TV all night long. Consequently, she never wants me to have any fun.
24. Six is an odd number of legs for a horse and two cannot divide an odd number. Hence, two cannot divide six.
25. This coffee has 99% less caffeine than regular coffee for it is 99% caffeine free.
26. Each part of the car must be 13 years old because the car is 13 years old.

NOTES

27. You must believe in God for anyone who does not believe in Him will spend the rest of eternity in the fires of Hell.
28. No one who has the slightest acquaintance with science could doubt that miracles such as those described in the Bible actually occurred, since every year we witness new miracles such as organ transplants, space exploration, and incredibly powerful microcomputers.
29. Nobody should be committed against his will to a mental institution because there is no real difference between insanity and eccentricity.
30. Either we leave the defense budget alone or we lose our status as a military power. No one wants to lose our status as a military power, so we must leave the defense budget alone.
31. There are more churches in New York City than in any other city in the U.S., and there are also more crimes in New York. Therefore, religious belief is a main cause of crime in America.

ANSWERS:

1. EQUIVOCATION ["end"]
2. CAUSAL SLIPPERY SLOPE
3. APPEAL TO COMMON PRACTICE
4. (Circumstantial) AD HOMINEM
5. QUESTIONABLE CAUSE
6. APPEAL TO POPULARITY
7. (Abusive) AD HOMINEM
8. SUPPRESSED EVIDENCE [Life expectancy has increased among *all* people during this same time period.]
9. EQUIVOCATION ["is," "love," "blind"]
10. TWO WRONGS MAKE A RIGHT
11. BEGGING THE QUESTION
12. APPEAL TO AUTHORITY
13. CAUSAL SLIPPERY SLOPE
14. VAGUENESS ["pornography"]
15. UNREPRESENTATIVE SAMPLE
16. DIVISION
17. APPEAL TO POPULARITY
18. UNREPRESENTATIVE SAMPLE
19. COMPOSITION
20. (Circumstantial) AD HOMINEM
21. FALSE DILEMMA [Suppressed dilemma]
22. APPEAL TO IGNORANCE
23. SMALL SAMPLE
24. EQUIVOCATION ["odd"]
25. QUESTIONABLE STATISTICS
26. DIVISION
27. APPEAL TO FORCE
28. EQUIVOCATION ["miracles"]
29. VAGUENESS ["insanity"]
30. FALSE DILEMMA
31. QUESTIONABLE CAUSE